The European Badger: A Comprehensive Study

J. McGarrity

ISBN:

DEDICATION

To Eleanor, who accompanied me on an enchanting woodland night, sharing the company of magical friends, and to Paul, whom I miss with every beat of my heart, now and forever. Lastly, to my son Owen, for joining me in the simple yet profound pleasure of watching the clouds drift by.

CONTENTS

ACKNOWLEDGMENTS

This book is dedicated to my late son, Paul, whose memory has been a constant source of strength and inspiration throughout the research and writing process. His presence has been dearly missed, but I hope that this work serves as a testament to the love and determination he instilled in me.

I am immensely grateful to my family, who have provided unwavering support, understanding, and encouragement as I embarked on this solitary journey. Their belief in me has given me the motivation needed to complete this project.

Finally, I extend my heartfelt thanks to the badgers themselves, whose fascinating lives and intriguing behaviours have provided the content and purpose for this book. It is my hope that the knowledge shared within these pages will contribute to a greater understanding and appreciation of these remarkable creatures.

This work is a culmination of my own dedication and passion, and I am grateful for the opportunity to share it with you, the reader. Thank you for joining me on this journey.

.

Chapter I: Introduction

© J. McGarrity.)

Author's Note:

"Many years ago, I ventured out with the hope of discovering a truly wild badger, determined to witness these elusive creatures thriving in their natural environment. After many days and hours spent scouring the countryside, I stumbled upon a badger sett. I positioned myself nearby, patiently awaiting the perfect moment.

The evening air was cool and moist, carrying the fragrance of blossoming flowers. I lay there for hours, the damp soil beneath me, as nature's symphony played all around. As the sun dipped below the horizon, anticipation swelled within me, knowing that the badgers would soon emerge. However, as darkness enveloped the area, apprehension crept in. I remained still, silently hoping that fortune would favour me.

Suddenly, I detected movement from the corner of my eye. Straining to see through the darkness, I tried to discern what was happening. As my eyes adapted to the low light, I realised a badger had exited the sett and was foraging just a few feet away. The sight of its fur glistening in the moonlight was mesmerising, and I found myself entranced by its every move. However, my delight was nearly spoiled by a magpie nesting in a nearby tree. I lay motionless, praying it wouldn't begin to shriek.

Time seemed to stand still as I silently observed the badger carrying on with its nightly routine. When the badger finally retreated into its sett, a wave of melancholy swept over me. The experience had passed, but the memory would remain eternally etched in my mind. That night, I departed the woods with a sense of gratitude and humility, profoundly moved by the splendour of the natural world. So began a lifelong passion for this enigmatic nocturnal enigma.

J. McGarrity."

I. Introduction

Badgers, members of the family Mustelidae, are captivating creatures that have intrigued humans for centuries. They inhabit a wide variety of habitats across Europe, Asia, and North America, playing essential ecological roles as predators, seed dispersers, and soil aerators. Their elusive nature and striking appearance have led to their prevalence in mythology, folklore, and literature. This book aims to provide a comprehensive overview of badgers, delving into their taxonomy, evolution, physical characteristics, distribution, habitat, diet, social structure, reproduction, ecology, conservation, cultural and historical significance, and the various threats they face.

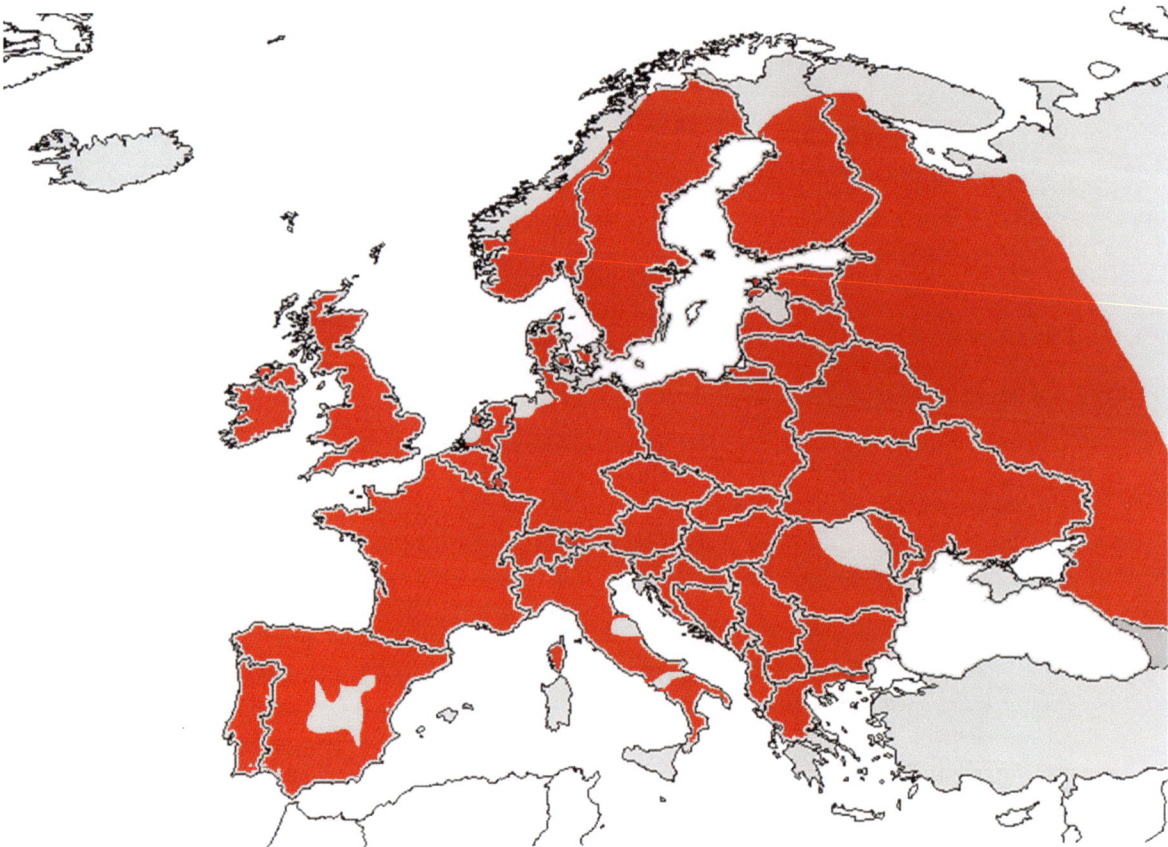

(The approximate distribution of the European badger (Meles meles) in Europe. Map based primarily on Michell-Jones et al. (1999) and IUCN data, modified according to Abramov et al. (2013) and Kinoshita et al. (2017). - Credit: Marc Baldwin.)

Understanding badgers' biology, ecology, and behaviour is crucial to their conservation, as it allows us to identify the factors that influence their survival and develop effective strategies to protect them. By exploring their taxonomy and evolution, we gain insights into the relationships between badger species, their adaptations to specific environments, and the pressures that have shaped their evolution.

The physical characteristics of badgers contribute not only to their unique appearance but also play a vital role in their survival. Examining their morphology helps us understand how badgers have adapted to their environments and the specific challenges they face.

Distribution and habitat are key factors in badgers' ecology and conservation. Knowing where badgers live and the types of habitats they occupy helps us identify areas most in need of conservation efforts and the impact of habitat loss, fragmentation, and climate change on their populations.

Badgers' diet and foraging behaviour have direct implications on their survival and their role within ecosystems. Studying their food sources and foraging strategies helps us understand their position in the food web, their interaction with other predators, and their vulnerability to changes in prey availability.

Social structure and behaviour are essential aspects of badgers' lives, affecting their reproduction, survival, and interactions with other species. A deeper understanding of their social systems, communication, territoriality, and interspecific interactions can inform conservation strategies targeting specific social or behavioural traits.

Chapter II: Taxonomy and Evolution

(© J. McGarrity.)

I. Introduction

The diverse and intriguing family of badgers belongs to the Mustelidae family, which includes other well-known members such as otters, weasels, and wolverines. Badgers exhibit a variety of characteristics and behaviours that have captured the fascination of humans for centuries. This section aims to explore the taxonomy and evolution of badgers, providing an in-depth look at their classification, species, and subspecies. We will also delve into the fossil record, examining the ancestral origins of these creatures and the factors that have influenced their divergence from other mustelids. Furthermore, we will discuss the adaptations that have enabled badgers to thrive in their respective habitats and touch on the prospects of their evolution. This comprehensive overview will provide readers with a solid understanding of the diverse and captivating world of badgers.

II. Classification and Species of Badgers

In the world of biology, a system known as scientific classification is used to categorize and organize living organisms according to their shared characteristics and evolutionary relationships. The European badger is no exception, and understanding its classification provides valuable insights into its place in the animal kingdom.

Kingdom: Animalia - The European badger belongs to the kingdom Animalia, which encompasses all multicellular, eukaryotic organisms that are characterised by their heterotrophic mode of nutrition, meaning they obtain nutrients by consuming other organisms.

Phylum: Chordata As a member of the phylum Chordata, the badger possesses a notochord, a dorsal nerve cord, pharyngeal slits, and a post-anal tail at some stage during its development. These features are common among chordates, which also include other mammals, birds, reptiles, amphibians, and fish.

Class: Mammalia the European badger is classified within the class Mammalia, which consists of warm-blooded, vertebrate animals characterised by the presence of hair or fur, mammary glands that produce milk to nourish their young, and a neocortex region in the brain.

Order: Carnivora Belonging to the order Carnivora, badgers share characteristics with other carnivorous mammals such as lions, bears, and seals. Carnivorans typically have specialised teeth adapted for slicing and tearing flesh, as well as a pair of specialised carnassial teeth.

Family: Mustelidae the European badger is part of the Mustelidae family, a diverse group of carnivorous mammals that includes other species such as weasels, otters, and wolverines. Mustelids are known for their elongated bodies, short legs, and anal scent glands, which they use for communication and territorial marking.

Genus: Meles Meles is the genus to which the European badger belongs, and it comprises three species of badgers native to Eurasia. Members of this genus share specific morphological and genetic traits that distinguish them from other badger species.

Species: Meles Meles Finally, the European badger's species name is Meles meles, denoting its unique combination of characteristics that set it apart from other members of the Meles genus and the wider Mustelidae family.

A. European Badger (Meles meles)

(Source wiki. © Unknown.)

Description: Medium-sized badger with a stocky body, short legs, and a characteristic black and white striped face. Fur is silvery-grey on the back and dark on the underparts.

Distribution: Found across most of Europe, extending into parts of western Asia.

Habitat: Deciduous and mixed woodlands, hedgerows, pastures, and agricultural areas.

Behaviour: Social, living in groups called "clans." Nocturnal, foraging mainly for earthworms and other invertebrates, but also known to eat small mammals, fruits, and roots.

B. American Badger (Taxidea taxus)

(Source wiki. © Unknown.)

Description: Medium-sized badger with a broad, flattened body, short legs, and a grizzled grey coat. The face is distinctively marked with black and white stripes.

Distribution: Found throughout central and western North America.

Habitat: Grasslands, prairies, and open woodlands.

Behaviour: Solitary, except during the mating season. Nocturnal, with a diverse diet consisting of rodents, insects, reptiles, and occasionally plant matter.

C. Asian Badger (Meles leucurus)

(Source wiki. © Unknown.)

Description: Similar in appearance to the European badger, but with a more elongated skull and a lighter coat colour.

Distribution: Occurs across northern Asia, from Siberia to China and Korea.

Habitat: Mixed and coniferous forests, meadows, and sometimes agricultural areas.

Behaviour: Social, living in groups similar to the European badger. Nocturnal, feeding on earthworms, insects, small mammals, and plant matter.

D. Japanese Badger (Meles anakuma)

(Japanese badger at Inokashira Park Zoo (Main park), Tokyo, on Sat 20 Jun 2009. © Unknown)

Description: Medium-sized badger with distinct facial markings, slightly smaller than European and Asian badgers.

Distribution: Found in Japan.

Habitat: Mixed and deciduous forests, grasslands, and sometimes agricultural areas.

Behaviour: Nocturnal, with a diet similar to other Meles species, including earthworms, insects, small mammals, and plant matter.

E. Honey Badger (Mellivora capensis)

(Honey badger at Satara camp in Kruger National Park, South Africa. © Unknown)

Description: Medium-sized, stocky badger with a distinctive black and white colouration. The upper part of the body is covered in coarse, light grey hair, while the lower part and legs are black.

Distribution: Found across sub-Saharan Africa, the Arabian Peninsula, and parts of western Asia and India.

Habitat: Semi-arid grasslands, savannas, and open woodlands.

Behaviour: Solitary and mostly nocturnal. Known for its fearlessness and tenacity, it has a diverse diet, including honey, insects, small mammals, reptiles, and carrion.

F. Stink Badgers (Mydaus javanensis and Mydaus marchei)

(Mydaus javanensis (Desmarest, 1820) - Sunda Stink Badger. © Klaus Rudloff.)

Description: Small, stocky badgers with a distinctive gland at the base of their tail that emits a pungent odour when threatened.

Distribution: Mydaus javanensis is found in Indonesia, while Mydaus marchei is native to the Philippines.

Habitat: Forests, grasslands, and agricultural areas.

Behaviour: Nocturnal and mainly terrestrial, they feed on invertebrates, small vertebrates, and plant material.

III. Comparison of Badger Species

A. Morphology

The species vary in size and colouration, with unique facial markings for each species. Honey badgers have a more elongated body compared to other badgers, while stink badgers possess a gland at the base of their tail for emitting a pungent odour.

B. Distribution

Badger species are distributed across Europe, Asia, Africa, and North America. European badgers (Meles meles) are found predominantly in Europe and parts of Western Asia. American badgers (Taxidea taxus) are native to central and western North America. Asian badgers (Meles leucurus) are found in Eastern Asia, spanning countries such as Russia, China, Mongolia, North Korea, and South Korea. Honey badgers (Mellivora capensis) are primarily distributed in sub-Saharan Africa, with their range extending to parts of western Asia and India. Lastly, stink badgers, which include the Palawan stink badger (Mydaus marchei) and the Sunda stink badger (Mydaus javanensis), are native to Indonesia and the Philippines.

C. Habitat

Badgers inhabit various ecosystems, including forests, grasslands, savannas, and agricultural areas. The specific habitat preference depends on the species; for example, American badgers prefer grasslands and prairies, while European badgers inhabit deciduous and mixed woodlands.

D. Behaviour

Badger species exhibit varying degrees of social behaviour. European and Asian badgers are social and live in groups called "clans," while American badgers, honey badgers, and stink badgers are primarily solitary. All badger species are nocturnal, with their diets consisting of invertebrates, small mammals, and plant material. However, honey badgers are known for their fearlessness and tenacity, often attacking larger prey and raiding bee nests for honey.

IV. Origins and Divergence

The evolutionary history of European badgers is a fascinating journey that traces back millions of years, highlighting the remarkable adaptations and divergence events that have shaped this species over time.

A. Ancestral Origins

The ancestors of modern badgers are believed to have originated in Asia during the early Miocene epoch, around 20 million years ago. These early mustelids diversified and migrated across various continents, giving rise to numerous lineages and species.

B. Divergence from Other Mustelids

The European badger (Meles meles) diverged from its closest relatives, the Asian badger (Meles leucurus) and the Japanese badger (Meles anakuma), around 4-6 million years ago. This divergence likely resulted from geographic isolation and subsequent genetic drift, leading to the distinct characteristics observed in each species today.

C. Climatic and Environmental Influences

Throughout their evolutionary history, badgers have adapted to various climatic and environmental conditions. These factors have played a significant role in shaping their behaviour, morphology, and distribution, ultimately leading to the emergence of the modern European badger.

D. Glacial Periods and Range Expansion

During the Pleistocene epoch, glacial periods significantly impacted the distribution and range of European badgers. As ice sheets retreated, badgers expanded their range into newly available habitats, allowing for greater genetic diversity and the formation of distinct populations.

V. Fossil Record

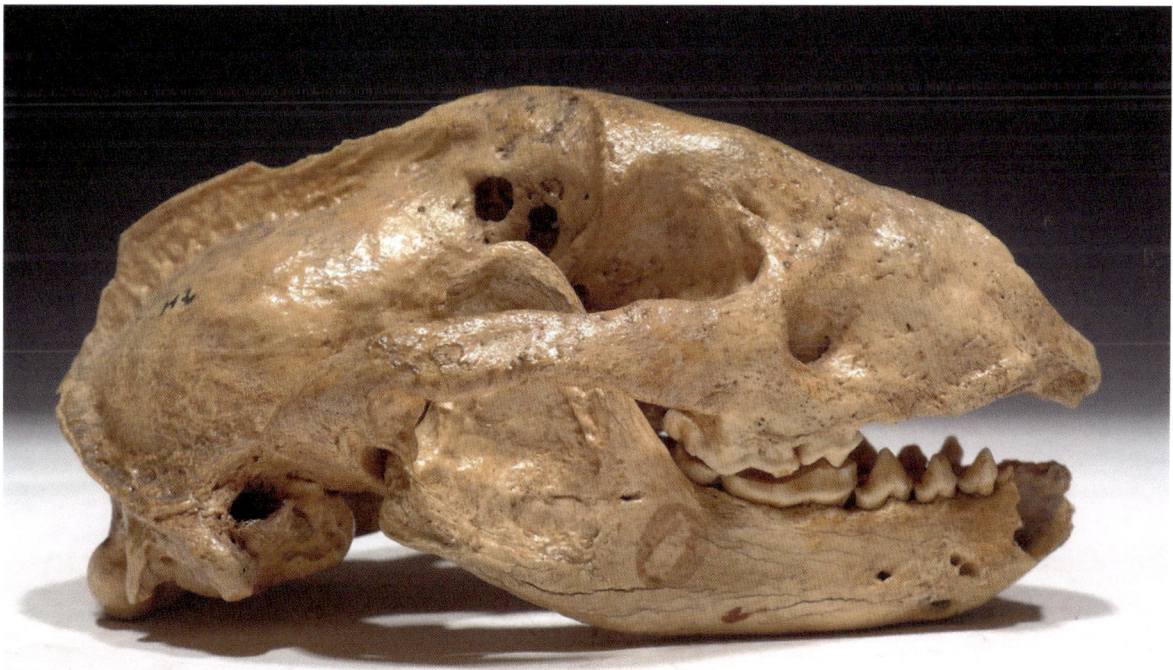

(Ice age fossil badger skull found in Belgian cave © Unknown)

The fossil record provides crucial insights into the evolutionary history of European badgers, revealing the changes and adaptations that have taken place over millions of years.

A. Early Mustelid Fossils

Fossils of early mustelids date back to the Oligocene epoch, providing evidence of the ancient origins of the badger lineage. The Oligocene is a geologic epoch of the Paleogene Period and extends from about

33.9 million to 23.03 million years before the present.

B. Emergence of Badger-like Species

During the Miocene epoch, fossils of early badger-like species began to appear, suggesting a divergence from other mustelids. The Miocene is the first geological epoch of the Neogene Period and extends from about 23.03 to 5.333 million years ago.

C. Pliocene and Pleistocene Fossils

Fossils from the Pliocene and Pleistocene epochs show further diversification of badger species and the emergence of more modern forms. The Pliocene is the epoch in the geologic time scale that extends from 5.333 million to 2.58 million years ago. The Pleistocene is the geological epoch that lasted from c. 2.58 million to 11,700 years ago, spanning the Earth's most recent period of repeated glaciations.

D. Extinct Badger Species

The fossil record also reveals the existence of extinct badger species, providing a broader context for understanding the evolution and diversification of this group.

VI. Subspecies Differentiation and Hybridization

Fossil evidence can be used to study the emergence of distinct subspecies, revealing how different populations adapted to local conditions. A. Morphological Changes Fossil evidence reveals changes in badger morphology over time, including adaptations in dentition and skeletal structure that allowed them to exploit different ecological niches. B. Distribution of Fossils The geographical distribution of badger fossils helps to shed light on the species' historical range, as well as past climate and habitat conditions. C. Palaeoenvironmental Context The study of fossils helps to reconstruct the past environments in which badgers lived, offering insights into how the species has responded to changing environmental conditions. D. Hybridisation Hybridisation is the process of interbreeding between different species or subspecies, resulting in the production of offspring that possess a combination of genetic traits from both parent populations. In the case of the European badger (Meles meles), there is limited evidence of XXXharacterized occurring between different subspecies or with other mustelids. This may be attributed to several factors, including the species' strong territoriality, specific habitat preferences, and distinct reproductive behaviours.

Within the European badger's range, it may occasionally share habitats with other closely related mustelids, such as the Asian badger (Meles leucurus) and the Japanese badger (Meles anakuma). However, natural XXXharacterized events between these species have not been documented. This is likely due to the significant differences in their geographical ranges, ecological niches, and breeding habits, which limit the opportunities for interbreeding.

Hybridisation between different subspecies of the European badger is also relatively rare, as the subspecies are generally isolated from one another by geographical barriers and habitat preferences. However, occasional contact between subspecies may occur at the edges of their respective ranges, potentially leading to limited gene flow between populations.

In summary, XXXharacterized in European badgers is not a common phenomenon, as the species and its subspecies are well-adapted to their specific environments and exhibit strong territorial behaviours. This low level of XXXharacterized helps maintain the genetic integrity of the species and its subspecies, ensuring the continued survival and evolution of this ecologically important mustelid.

VII. Phylogenetics and Genetic Research

A. Phylogenetic Methods

Phylogenetics is the study of the evolutionary relationships among species, which is crucial in understanding the taxonomy and evolution of badgers. Several methods have been developed to construct phylogenetic trees, including Maximum Parsimony, Maximum Likelihood, Bayesian Inference, Distance-based methods, and Gene-tree reconciliation. These methods use different algorithms and criteria to infer the most likely evolutionary relationships among species based on molecular and morphological data.

B. Genetic Research Techniques

Genetic research has greatly advanced our understanding of badger evolution, taxonomy, and ecology. Key techniques employed in genetic studies include DNA sequencing, population genetics, phylogeography, molecular markers, and genomics. These methods have provided insights into badger population structure, gene flow, and the genetic basis of adaptation, among other aspects.

C. Conservation Genetics

Conservation genetics focuses on the application of genetic research to the conservation of species. For badgers, this includes assessing levels of genetic diversity and population structure, identifying genetically distinct populations, and understanding the impacts of habitat fragmentation on gene flow. This information is vital for informing effective conservation strategies and management plans.

D. Disease Ecology

Genetic research has also played a significant role in understanding the disease ecology of badgers, particularly in relation to their role as reservoirs for diseases such as bovine tuberculosis. Studies have investigated the genetic basis of disease susceptibility and resistance in badgers, as well as the transmission dynamics and host-pathogen interactions. This knowledge is crucial for developing effective disease control and management strategies.

E. Comparative Genomics

Comparative genomics involves the comparison of genomes from different species to identify similarities and differences in their genetic makeup. This approach has been employed to study badger evolution and their relationships with other mustelids. By comparing the genomes of various badger species and other related taxa, researchers can gain insights into the molecular basis of their unique adaptations, as well as the evolutionary forces shaping their diversification.

VIII. Adaptations

Badgers exhibit a range of adaptations that have allowed them to thrive in diverse environments and ecological niches. These adaptations can be categorized into various aspects of their biology, behaviour, and physiology.

A. Burrow Construction

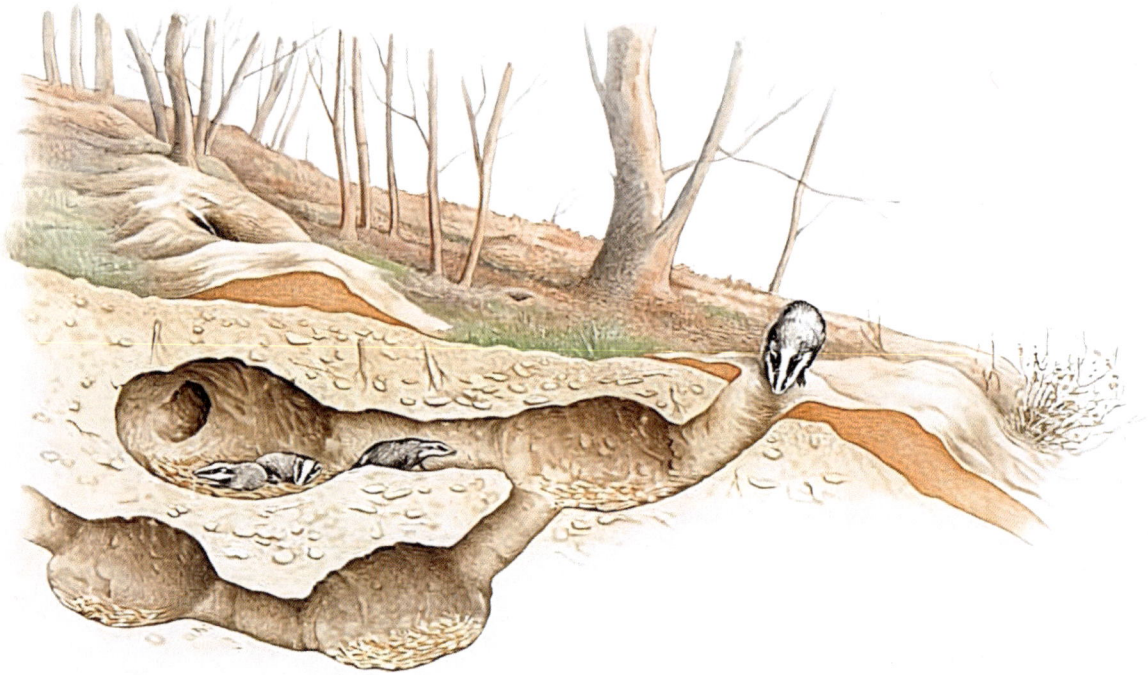

(© gettyimages)

One of the most notable adaptations of badgers is their ability to construct elaborate burrow systems, called setts. These setts provide shelter, protection from predators, and a place for raising young. Badgers have powerful forelimbs and long, strong claws, which enable them to dig efficiently through various soil types.

(© gettyimages)

B. Nocturnal Lifestyle

Badgers are primarily nocturnal, which is an adaptation that helps them avoid predators and minimize competition with other species for resources. Their nocturnal lifestyle is supported by adaptations such as enhanced night vision and sensitive whiskers (vibrissae) that aid in navigation and foraging in low light conditions.

C. Omnivorous Diet

Badgers have an omnivorous diet, consuming a wide variety of plant and animal matter, including invertebrates, small mammals, fruits, and roots. This dietary flexibility enables them to exploit diverse food sources and adapt to changing resource availability in their environment.

D. Camouflage

The distinctive black and white facial markings of badgers serve as a form of camouflage, helping them blend in with their surroundings and avoid detection by predators. This colouration also acts as a warning signal, indicating to potential predators that badgers are a formidable opponent.

E. Body Shape

Badgers have a stocky, low-slung body shape that is well-suited for navigating through their burrows and under dense vegetation. This compact form also provides them with increased stability and leverage when digging.

F. Social Structure

Some badger species exhibit a social structure that involves group living, which can provide benefits such as increased foraging efficiency, communal care of offspring, and improved predator defence. This social organization is supported by adaptations for scent communication, which helps to maintain group cohesion and coordinate behaviours.

G. Seasonal Adaptations

Badgers have developed various seasonal adaptations, such as fat storage during periods of resource abundance, delayed implantation of fertilized eggs, and counter-current heat exchange systems to regulate body temperature during colder months. These adaptations enable them to survive and reproduce in fluctuating environmental conditions.

By understanding the various adaptations of badgers, we gain a deeper appreciation for the evolutionary processes that have shaped these unique and fascinating creatures.

IX. Relations to Other Mustelids

Badgers belong to the family Mustelidae, which includes a diverse range of carnivorous mammals such as otters, weasels, ferrets, martens, and wolverines. While badgers share some characteristics with these other mustelids, they also exhibit unique adaptations that set them apart. Understanding the relationships between badgers and other mustelids can provide valuable insights into their evolutionary history and ecological roles.

A. Shared Characteristics

Badgers share certain traits with other mustelids, including a well-developed sense of smell, elongated bodies, and XXXharacteriz dentition for carnivory. Like many mustelids, badgers have scent glands that produce strong-smelling secretions used for communication and territorial marking.

B. Evolutionary Relationships

Phylogenetic analyses have shed light on the evolutionary relationships among badgers and other mustelids. These studies suggest that badgers diverged from a common ancestor with other mustelids around 18-20 million years ago. The specific relationships among badger species and their position within the mustelid family tree remain an active area of research, with new molecular data and phylogenetic methods continuing to refine our understanding of their evolutionary history.

C. Divergence from Other Mustelids

Badgers have evolved several unique adaptations that differentiate them from other mustelids, such as their fossorial lifestyle, nocturnal habits, and in some cases, social structure. These adaptations have allowed badgers to occupy ecological niches that are distinct from those of their mustelid relatives, reducing competition for resources and enabling them to coexist in shared environments.

D. Ecological Niche Partitioning

Badgers and other mustelids have evolved to occupy different ecological niches, which helps minimize competition for resources. For example, while badgers primarily forage on the ground for invertebrates and small mammals, otters are XXXharacteriz for aquatic environments, and martens are adapted for arboreal lifestyles. This niche partitioning allows multiple mustelid species to coexist in the same ecosystems.

E. Convergent Evolution

In some cases, badgers and other mustelids have independently evolved similar traits in response to similar ecological pressures, a phenomenon known as convergent evolution. For instance, the elongated body shape and XXXharacteriz digging adaptations seen in badgers have also evolved in the American badger, reflecting the shared fossorial lifestyle of these species by exploring the relationships between badgers and other mustelids, we can gain a greater understanding of the evolutionary processes that have shaped these diverse and fascinating mammals.

X. Subspecies of Meles meles

The European badger (Meles meles) is a widespread and adaptable species, with its range extending across much of Europe and parts of Asia. Due to this extensive distribution and the resulting variation in local environmental conditions, several subspecies of Meles meles have been identified. These subspecies exhibit differences in morphology, coat colouration, and other characteristics that reflect their adaptation to specific habitats and geographic regions.

A. Meles meles meles

Meles meles meles is the nominate subspecies, found across a large part of the European badger's range. It is XXXharacterized by a relatively large body size and the classic black and white facial markings, with a distinctive white stripe running from the nose to the ears.

B. Meles meles marianensis

Meles meles marianensis is a subspecies found in the Iberian Peninsula, primarily in Spain and Portugal. This subspecies tends to be smaller in size and has a lighter coat colouration compared to the nominate subspecies. The facial markings are less distinct, with the white stripe often being less prominent or even absent.

C. Meles meles canescens

Meles meles canescens occurs in the eastern part of the European badger's range, particularly in parts of Russia and Asia. This subspecies exhibits a lighter coat color and a more extensive white area on the head, with the white stripe sometimes extending onto the back of the neck.

D. Meles meles heptneri

Meles meles heptneri is found in the southeastern part of the species' range, including areas of Iran, Afghanistan, and Pakistan. This subspecies is XXXharacterized by a relatively small body size and a coat color that is generally darker than that of other subspecies. The white facial stripe is typically more distinct and may extend further onto the back of the neck.

These subspecies of Meles meles highlight the remarkable adaptability of the European badger, as well as the importance of understanding the genetic diversity within species for effective conservation efforts. Future research may uncover additional subspecies or refine our understanding of the relationships among existing subspecies as new genetic data and analytical methods become available.

XI. Future Evolutionary Prospects

The future evolutionary prospects of the European badger (Meles meles) are subject to a variety of factors, including environmental changes, human influences, and the species' inherent adaptability. As badgers continue to adapt to shifting habitats and ecological pressures, it is likely that new subspecies may emerge and the range of existing subspecies may change over time.

1. Environmental factors

Climate change is a significant factor that can affect the future evolution of the European badger. As temperatures rise and precipitation patterns change, badgers may be forced to adapt to new environmental conditions or shift their ranges to find suitable habitats. This could potentially lead to the development of new subspecies or the extinction of existing ones.

2. Human influence

Human activities, such as habitat destruction, road construction, and agricultural practices, can also affect the future evolution of badgers. As habitats become fragmented or degraded, badger populations may become isolated, potentially leading to the development of new subspecies or inbreeding within isolated populations. Conservation efforts to protect badger habitats and maintain connectivity among populations will be crucial to preserving the species' genetic diversity and evolutionary potential.

Adaptability

Badgers have proven to be highly adaptable animals, capable of surviving in various habitats and adjusting to changing environmental conditions. This adaptability may be an important factor in their future evolution, as it enables badgers to persist in the face of environmental challenges and exploit new ecological niches. As badgers continue to adapt, it is likely that their morphology, behaviour, and ecological roles will also evolve.

4. Genetic research and conservation

Advancements in genetic research can provide valuable insights into the evolutionary history and future prospects of the European badger. By studying the genetic variation within and between populations, researchers can better understand the factors that drive evolutionary change and inform conservation strategies to protect the species and its genetic diversity.

In summary, the future evolutionary prospects of the European badger will be shaped by a combination of environmental factors, human influences, and the species' inherent adaptability. While it is impossible to predict the exact course of badger evolution, understanding these factors and promoting conservation efforts can help ensure the continued survival and diversity of this remarkable species.

XII. Summary and Conclusion

In conclusion, the European badger (Meles meles) has a rich evolutionary history, XXXharacterized by its adaptability and resilience in the face of changing environmental conditions and human influences. Throughout its taxonomy and evolution, the species has exhibited remarkable morphological, behavioural, and ecological diversity, reflecting its ability to exploit a wide range of habitats and resources.

Phylogenetic and genetic research has provided valuable insights into the relationships between badgers and other mustelids, as well as the factors that have shaped the species' evolutionary history. The study of badger adaptations has further revealed the myriad ways in which these animals have evolved to thrive in their environments, from burrow construction and nocturnal behaviour to social structure and scent communication.

The future evolutionary prospects of the European badger will be influenced by ongoing environmental changes, human activities, and the species' inherent adaptability. By understanding these factors and promoting conservation efforts, we can help protect the genetic diversity and evolutionary potential of this fascinating species.

Ultimately, the study of the European badger's taxonomy and evolution offers valuable lessons in the importance of adaptability, diversity, and conservation for the continued survival and success of the species. As we deepen our understanding of the factors that have shaped the badger's past and present, we can better prepare to face the challenges and opportunities that lie ahead in its future evolution.

Chapter III: Physical Characteristics

(The forepaw of a European badger. Source wiki. © Unknown.)

I. Introduction

Badgers, belonging to the family Mustelidae, are an intriguing group of mammals characterised by their unique physical adaptations that enable them to thrive in diverse habitats. The study of their physical characteristics not only provides valuable insights into their biology and ecology but also helps us understand their relationships with other mustelids and the various factors that have shaped their evolution. In this chapter, we will explore the various physical features of badgers, including their body structure, fur and colouration, head and facial features, dentition, limbs and locomotion, scent glands, and unique adaptations. Additionally, we will compare the anatomy of badgers with other mustelids to highlight the similarities and differences that make them distinct within the animal kingdom.

(© J. McGarrity)

II. Body Structure and Size

A. Size and Weight

Badgers exhibit a robust body structure with a stocky build and a low centre of gravity, which helps them navigate their terrestrial habitats efficiently. The size and weight of badgers vary depending on their species, age, and sex. Adult European badgers (Meles meles) typically measure between 60 to 90 cm in length and weigh between 8 and 12 kg, while American badgers (Taxidea taxus) have a slightly smaller size range of 42 to 76 cm and weigh between 4 and 12 kg. The smaller species, such as the Asian badgers (Meles anakuma and Meles amurensis), have an average body length of 50 to 70 cm and weigh between 3 and 8 kg.

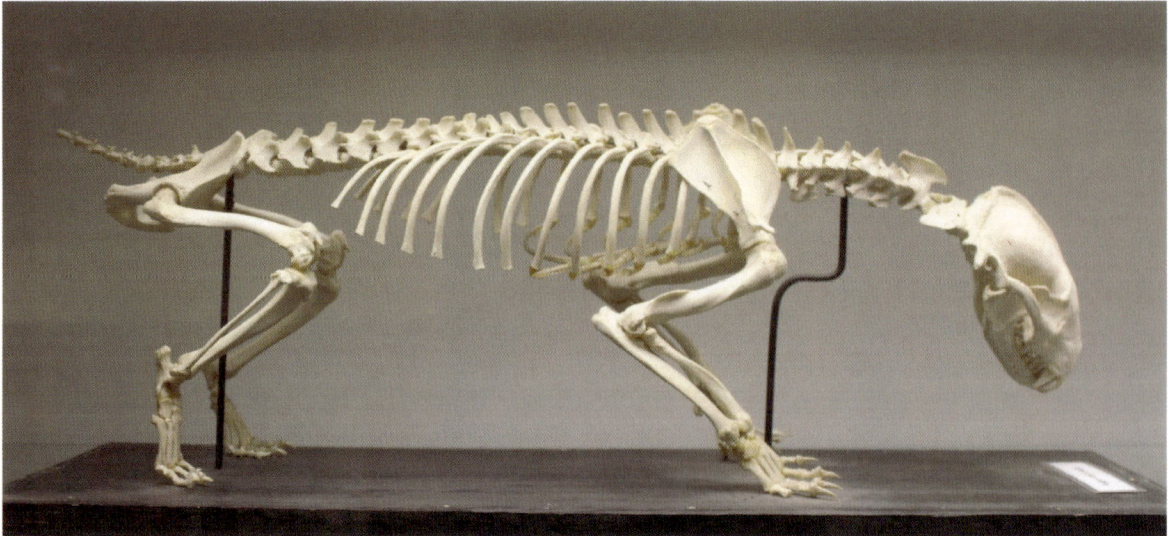

(European badger (Meles meles) skeleton at the Royal Veterinary College anatomy museum. © Mrjohncummings)

B. Sexual Dimorphism

Badgers exhibit sexual dimorphism, with males tending to be larger and heavier than females. This size difference is more pronounced in some species, such as the European and American badgers, where males can be up to 20% larger than females. The variation in size between the sexes is related to the mating system and competition among males for access to females during the breeding season.

C. Age-related Changes

Badger size and weight also vary with age, with juveniles being smaller and lighter than adults. As badgers grow and develop, their body structure becomes more robust, and their limbs and muscles become stronger to support their burrowing and foraging activities. In older individuals, signs of wear and tear on the body, such as worn teeth and reduced muscle mass, may become apparent, reflecting the challenges of a life spent in a physically demanding environment.

III. Fur and Colouration

A. Fur

Badgers have dense fur that serves multiple purposes, including thermoregulation, camouflage, and protection from the elements. The fur consists of two layers: a soft, insulating underfur and a coarse, protective outer layer known as guard hairs. The underfur provides insulation, helping badgers maintain a stable body temperature in various climatic conditions, while the guard hairs protect them from moisture, dirt, and abrasion.

B. Colouration

Badgers exhibit diverse colouration patterns across different species. The European badger, for instance, has a distinct black and white striped face, with greyish-brown fur covering the body and legs. The American badger has a lighter brownish-grey coat with a bold white stripe running from the nose to the back of the head. Asian badgers often have a greyish-brown coat with a darker mid-dorsal stripe and lighter underparts. The honey badger, a distinct species not closely related to the other badgers, has a unique black and white colouration pattern, with a stark white upper body and black lower body, legs, and face.

C. Camouflage and Signalling

The colouration patterns of badgers not only serve as camouflage but also play a role in signalling and communication. The contrasting facial markings of some species, such as the European badger, may serve as a warning to potential predators, signalling their tenacity and ability to defend themselves. Moreover, the markings can help individuals recognize each other during social interactions, facilitating the maintenance of their complex social structure.

D. Seasonal Variations

In some species, the fur colour and thickness may change seasonally. Badgers inhabiting colder climates typically have thicker fur during the winter months to help insulate them against the harsh temperatures. The fur may also become paler or darker, depending on the season, to better blend in with the changing environment.

E. Dentition

Badgers have a robust and specialised dentition adapted to their omnivorous diet. They possess a total of 34 teeth, including sharp canines for catching and holding prey, and strong molars for crushing and grinding plant material. The carnassial teeth, which are typical of carnivores, are less specialised in badgers, reflecting their diverse diet.

F. Health and Injuries

The physical condition of a badger's fur can provide important clues about its overall health. Healthy badgers typically have clean, well-groomed fur, while sick or injured individuals may display matted or dirty fur. Injuries, such as bite marks or scratches, can be visible on the fur, providing insights into recent conflicts or interactions with other animals.

G. Reproductive Status

Fur colouration and thickness can also be indicative of an individual's reproductive status. In some species, sexually mature males develop a thickened, darker patch of fur around their necks during the breeding season, which may help them assert dominance and attract mates.

H. Comparative Anatomy with Other Mustelids

While badgers share some similarities with other members of the mustelid family, such as weasels and otters, they also possess unique anatomical features that set them apart. These differences include a stockier body, shorter limbs, and a more powerful jaw, all of which are adaptations to their fossorial lifestyle and diverse diet.

I. Summary and Conclusion

Badgers exhibit a range of physical characteristics that reflect their unique adaptations, habitat preferences, and social behaviours. Their dense fur and distinct colouration patterns not only provide insulation and camouflage but also play a role in signalling and communication. By comparing badgers' anatomy to that of other mustelids, we can better understand the ecological niches they occupy and the evolutionary processes that have shaped their distinctive features.

IV. Head and Facial Features

(© unknown)

Badgers possess a distinctive head shape and facial features that set them apart from other mustelids. Their skull is relatively large and robust, with a strong, wide zygomatic arch to support powerful jaw muscles. The snout is elongated and somewhat wedge-shaped snout, which allows them to dig and forage efficiently in soil and undergrowth.

One of the most striking features of badgers is their characteristic facial markings. Most species have a black and white striped pattern on their faces, which extends from the nose to the back of the head. These contrasting stripes may serve several purposes, such as camouflage, communication, and recognition among individuals within a social group.

Badgers have small, rounded ears that are set low on the sides of their head. This feature helps to keep dirt and debris out while they are digging and burrowing. Their eyes are also relatively small, which reflects their nocturnal lifestyle and reliance on other senses, such as smell and touch, for navigation and foraging.

Whiskers, or vibrissae, are another important facial feature in badgers. These long, sensitive hairs are found around the snout, cheeks, and above the eyes, and provide them with a heightened sense of touch. Vibrissae play a crucial role in helping badgers navigate their environment, detect prey, and communicate with other members of their social group.

VI. Limbs and Locomotion

(© Unknown)

Badgers have sturdy, well-adapted limbs that enable them to navigate their environment efficiently. Their legs are relatively short and muscular, providing them with stability and strength, particularly when digging and burrowing. The forelimbs, in particular, are highly adapted for digging, with long, strong claws that allow badgers to excavate soil and create burrows with ease.

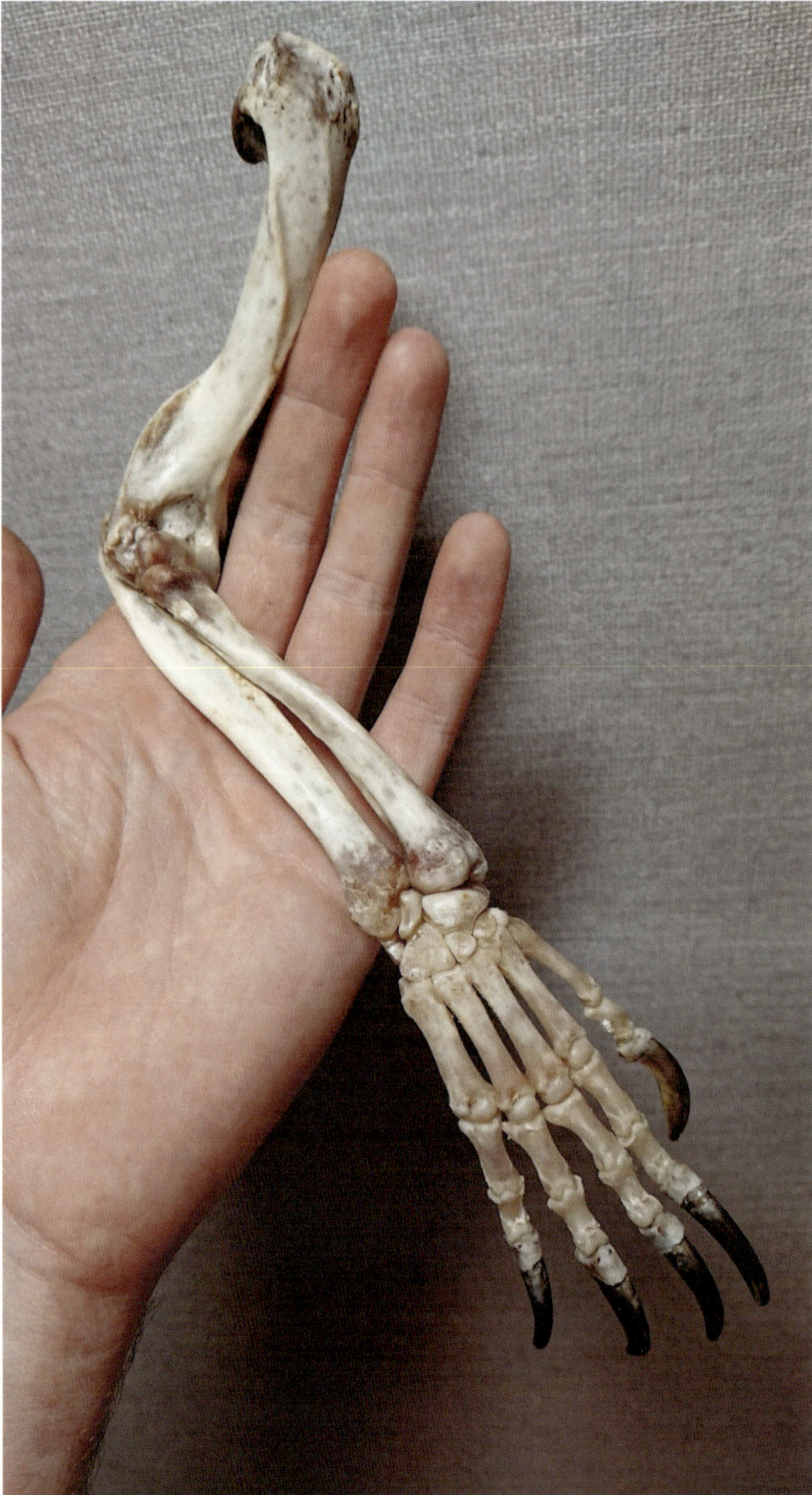

(Source reddit ©Posted by u/07Stocka.)

Their feet are of a plantigrade type, meaning that they walk with their entire foot touching the ground, as opposed to walking on their toes like many other animals. This provides them with added stability and traction, especially when moving through uneven terrain. The soles of their feet are also thick and padded, which helps to protect them from injury and provides additional grip.

Badgers are not known for their speed, but they can move quickly when necessary. Their powerful limbs enable them to sprint short distances, especially when escaping from predators or pursuing prey. However, their primary mode of locomotion is a slow, deliberate walk or trot, which is well-suited to their foraging and burrowing activities.

Despite their stocky build and short legs, badgers are also surprisingly agile climbers and swimmers. They are capable of scaling trees, fences, and other obstacles when searching for food or evading threats, and they have been known to swim across rivers and other bodies of water when necessary. These additional modes of locomotion provide badgers with greater versatility and adaptability in their natural habitats.

VII. Scent Glands and Communication

Scent glands play a crucial role in badger communication, helping them convey information to other members of their social group and marking their territories. Badgers possess a pair of anal glands, which secrete a strong, musky odour. This scent is unique to each individual and serves as a form of identification among badgers.

When marking their territories, badgers will frequently engage in a behaviour known as 'scent marking'. This involves rubbing their anal glands on the ground, tree trunks, or other prominent features in the landscape to establish their presence and deter rival badgers from entering the territory. Scent marking also plays a role in mating, with males using their scent to attract females during the breeding season.

In addition to their anal glands, badgers also have a series of smaller scent glands located around their faces, particularly near the eyes and ears. These glands produce secretions that are used to convey social information, such as dominance status, to other members of their group. Badgers will often engage in mutual grooming and scent rubbing, where they rub their faces and bodies against one another to exchange scent information and reinforce social bonds.

Badgers also communicate using a range of vocalisations, including growls, chatters, and high-pitched whistles. While these vocalisations are not as prominent as scent communication, they do play an essential role in maintaining social harmony within the group and warning other badgers of potential threats or dangers.

In summary, scent glands and communication are critical aspects of badger biology, allowing them to maintain their complex social structures and interactions within their communities.

VIII. Unique Adaptations

Badgers possess several unique adaptations that enable them to thrive in their specific environments and ecological niches. Some of these adaptations include:

1. Burrow construction: Badgers are exceptional diggers, thanks to their powerful forelimbs and long, sturdy claws. They create complex burrow systems called 'setts', which provide them with shelter, protection from predators, and a place to raise their young. Setts can be centuries old and are often shared by multiple generations of badgers.

2. Nocturnal lifestyle: Badgers are primarily nocturnal animals, which means they are most active during the night. This adaptation allows them to avoid many daytime predators and competition for resources.

3. Omnivorous diet: Badgers have a diverse and adaptable diet, which enables them to exploit a wide range of food sources. They are opportunistic feeders, consuming a variety of invertebrates, small mammals, birds, fruit, and plant material, depending on availability and season.

4. Delayed implantation: Female badgers exhibit a reproductive adaptation called 'delayed implantation', wherein fertilised eggs do not implant in the uterus immediately after fertilisation. Instead, they remain dormant for several months before implanting and developing into embryos. This adaptation allows badgers to time the birth of their young to coincide with favourable environmental conditions, ensuring a higher chance of survival.

5. Camouflage: The distinctive black and white facial markings of badgers serve as a form of camouflage, known as 'disruptive colouration'. This pattern breaks up the badger's outline, making it more challenging for predators to detect them, especially in low light conditions.

6. Counter-current heat exchange: Badgers have a unique circulatory adaptation in their paws called 'counter-current heat exchange', which helps them maintain a stable body temperature in cold environments. This system allows warm blood flowing to the extremities to exchange heat with the cold blood returning to the body, minimising heat loss and preventing frostbite.

These unique adaptations have allowed badgers to thrive in a variety of environments and habitats, contributing to their success as a species.

IX. Comparative Anatomy with Other Mustelids

Badgers belong to the Mustelidae family, which also includes otters, weasels, martens, and wolverines. While badgers share some similarities with other mustelids, they also possess several distinct anatomical features that set them apart from their relatives. Some of these differences are:

1. Body size: Badgers generally have a stockier and more robust body compared to other mustelids. This build allows them to be efficient diggers and provides them with the strength required for their burrowing lifestyle.

2. Limbs and locomotion: Badgers have shorter, stronger limbs with elongated claws, particularly on their forelimbs. These adaptations enable them to dig more effectively than most other mustelids. In contrast, some mustelids like otters and minks have elongated, slender bodies with webbed feet, which aid them in swimming and diving.

3. Fur and colouration: Badger fur is coarse and dense, providing them with insulation against the cold and wet conditions of their environments. Their characteristic black and white facial markings serve as disruptive colouration, offering camouflage in low light conditions. Other mustelids typically have more uniform colouration, ranging from dark brown to greyish tones.

4. Facial features: Badgers have a distinctively shaped head with a broad, triangular profile, and small, rounded ears. Their powerful jaws and large canines enable them to tackle a variety of food sources. Other mustelids, such as weasels, have longer, more slender snouts and smaller teeth, which are better suited to capturing and consuming small prey.

5. Scent glands: All mustelids possess scent glands, but the specific function and location of these glands vary among species. Badgers have anal glands located near the base of their tail, which they use for territorial marking and communication. In contrast, otters have scent glands near their anus, while skunks have well-developed anal glands that produce a potent defensive spray.

These comparative anatomical differences highlight the diversity within the Mustelidae family, with each species adapted to its specific ecological niche and behavioural traits.

X. Summary and Conclusion

In summary, badgers exhibit a variety of distinctive physical characteristics that set them apart from other mustelids. Their robust body structure, specialised limbs and claws, unique fur and colouration, and characteristic facial features all contribute to their adaptability and success in their natural habitats. Furthermore, their scent glands play a crucial role in communication and territorial marking, adding to their complex social structure.

Comparative anatomy with other mustelids demonstrates the remarkable diversity within the Mustelidae family, as each species is uniquely adapted to its specific ecological niche and behavioural requirements. Understanding these physical differences and their functional significance is essential for developing effective conservation strategies and protecting these fascinating creatures for future generations.

Chapter IV: Distribution and Habitat

(© J. McGarrity)

I. Introduction

In this chapter, we will explore the distribution and habitat preferences of badgers, focusing primarily on the European badger (Meles meles). Badgers are widely distributed across Europe and parts of Asia, occupying a diverse range of habitats. Understanding their distribution and habitat preferences is essential for conserving these charismatic mammals and ensuring their continued survival in the face of various environmental and human-induced challenges. We will delve into the historical distribution of badgers, the specific features that make certain habitats suitable for them, and their population density in these areas. Furthermore, we will discuss the factors affecting the expansion and contraction of their range, including human-induced changes, habitat fragmentation, and climate change. Finally, we will examine the interactions between badgers and other species, particularly their role as habitat engineers, and summarise the key points covered in this chapter.

II. Overview of Badger Distribution

Badgers exhibit a wide distribution across Europe and parts of Asia, with the European badger (Meles meles) being the most widespread species. Their range spans from the British Isles and the Iberian Peninsula in the west, to Russia and parts of Western Asia in the east, and from Scandinavia in the north to the Mediterranean region in the south. Within these areas, badgers can be found in a variety of habitats, including deciduous and mixed forests, grasslands, heathlands, and even urban environments.

In addition to the European badger, other badger species have distinct distribution patterns. The American badger (Taxidea taxus) is found predominantly in North America, whereas the Asian badgers (Meles anakuma and Meles amurensis) are native to East Asia. The Asian badger (Meles leucurus) occurs in parts of Western Asia and Eastern Europe, and the Honey badger (Mellivora capensis) is widely distributed across Africa and parts of Asia. Lastly, the Stink badgers (Mydaus javanensis and Mydaus marchei) inhabit parts of Southeast Asia, specifically Indonesia and the Philippines.

Understanding badger distribution patterns is crucial for implementing appropriate conservation measures and assessing the impacts of environmental changes on their populations.

III. Habitat Types and Suitability

Badgers are highly adaptable and can be found in a variety of habitat types across their distribution range. Some of the most common habitats include:

1. Deciduous and mixed forests: These habitats provide ample cover, food resources, and suitable sites for sett construction. In such environments, badgers often feed on earthworms, insects, small mammals, and seasonal fruits.

(Woodland at Pontypool in Wales © Unknown)

2. Grasslands and meadows: Open grasslands offer a rich supply of earthworms and insects, which form the primary diet of badgers. Additionally, these habitats provide suitable locations for foraging and sett construction, particularly when adjacent to woodlands or hedgerows.

(Alpine meadows, Grassland © Unknown)

(Grassland and meadow © Unknown)

3. Heathlands and moorlands: While these habitats may not be as rich in food resources as forests and grasslands, badgers can still thrive in these environments, provided there are sufficient areas of woodland or scrub for sett construction.

(© RODGER SLAPE)

(Heath and Moorland in Southern England © Unknown)

4. Farmland and agricultural areas: Badgers often find refuge in hedgerows, field margins, and woodland patches within agricultural landscapes. These areas provide shelter and food, particularly earthworms and small mammals.

(Farmland and agricultural © Unknown)

(Farmland and agricultural © Unknown)

5. Urban and suburban areas: As adaptable creatures, badgers can also be found in urban and suburban environments, particularly in parks, gardens, and other green spaces. They may use man-made structures for sett construction, such as underneath sheds or in embankments.

(European Badger (Meles meles) on the North Downs above Folkestone. Kent, UK, June. Camera trap photo ©
www.naturepl.com)

Badgers typically prefer habitats with a mosaic of different land cover types, providing a diverse range of resources and optimal foraging opportunities. Key features that make a habitat suitable for badgers include the presence of suitable sett construction sites, an abundant supply of food resources, and sufficient cover to avoid predation and disturbance.

IV. Range Expansion and Contraction

Badger populations have experienced both range expansion and contraction over time due to various factors, including climate fluctuations, human activities, and habitat changes.

1. Historical fluctuations: Throughout history, badger populations have experienced natural range fluctuations due to climatic events such as ice ages, which restricted their distribution to specific refugia. As the climate warmed and ice retreated, badgers expanded their range, colonising new areas and adapting to different habitats.

2. Human-induced range changes: Human activities have significantly impacted badger distribution, with both negative and positive consequences. Habitat loss, persecution, and hunting led to the contraction of badger populations in some areas, while legal protection and conservation efforts have facilitated range expansion in others.

3. Habitat loss and fragmentation: The conversion of natural habitats to agricultural land, urban development, and infrastructure has resulted in the loss and fragmentation of badger habitats. These changes have led to localised population declines and, in some cases, range contraction.

4. Persecution and hunting: In some regions, badgers have been persecuted or hunted for sport, fur, and as a means of pest control. These activities have led to population declines and range contraction, particularly where persecution was intense and sustained.

5. Indirect effects: Changes in the distribution and abundance of prey species or competitors due to human activities, habitat changes, or other factors can also influence badger populations, leading to range expansion or contraction.

6. Climate change: Climate change is likely to have a significant impact on badger distribution in the future. Warmer temperatures and altered precipitation patterns may result in range shifts, with some populations expanding into previously unsuitable areas, while others may contract due to unfavourable conditions.

Conservation efforts, such as habitat restoration and legal protection, have played a crucial role in promoting range expansion and stabilising badger populations in some areas. Understanding the factors influencing range dynamics is essential for effective management and conservation of badger populations.

V. Climate Change Impacts

Climate change is expected to have a range of impacts on badger populations, affecting their distribution, habitat, and behaviour. Some of the key climate change-related factors influencing badgers include:

1. Altered precipitation patterns: Changes in precipitation patterns, including more frequent extreme weather events such as droughts and heavy rainfall, can impact badger populations by affecting the availability and distribution of their food resources, as well as the quality and stability of their habitats.

2. Temperature changes: Rising temperatures may have both direct and indirect effects on badgers. Warmer conditions could lead to physiological stress, particularly during heatwaves, potentially affecting survival rates. Additionally, higher temperatures can influence the abundance and distribution of prey species, leading to changes in badger foraging behaviour and, ultimately, their distribution.

3. Changes in vegetation and habitats: Climate change can alter the distribution and composition of plant communities, affecting the structure and quality of badger habitats. This may impact the availability of suitable denning sites and food resources, resulting in shifts in badger distribution.

4. Disease prevalence: Climate change may affect the prevalence and distribution of diseases affecting badgers and their prey, such as bovine tuberculosis or other pathogens. Warmer temperatures and altered precipitation patterns can create conditions that favour the spread of certain diseases, which may have negative impacts on badger populations.

5. Adaptation and resilience: The ability of badger populations to adapt to climate change will depend on their resilience and adaptive capacity. Factors such as genetic diversity, habitat connectivity, and behavioural plasticity will influence how well badgers can respond to changing environmental conditions.

6. Range shifts and fragmentation: As the climate changes, badgers may shift their ranges in response to altered environmental conditions. This could lead to the expansion of badger populations into new areas or the contraction of their range in others. Range shifts can also result in increased fragmentation of populations, which may have implications for genetic diversity and long-term population viability.

Mitigating the impacts of climate change on badger populations will require the implementation of effective conservation strategies, such as habitat restoration, connectivity enhancement, and monitoring of population trends. Understanding and predicting the potential effects of climate change on badgers will be crucial for ensuring their long-term survival and conservation.

VI. Interactions with Other Species

Badgers interact with a variety of other species within their ecosystem, playing important roles in maintaining ecological balance and functioning. Some key interactions between badgers and other species include:

1. Predation and prey relationships: Badgers are omnivorous, with a diet consisting of a range of invertebrates, small mammals, birds, amphibians, and plant material. As predators, they help control the populations of certain prey species, such as earthworms, insects, and small mammals. Conversely, badgers themselves can fall prey to larger predators, such as wolves, lynxes, and bears, in some regions.

2. Competition: Badgers may compete with other species for resources such as food and shelter. For example, they may compete with foxes, pine martens, and other mustelids for access to small mammal prey or denning sites. In some cases, badgers may displace other species from their dens or occupy abandoned burrows.

3. Mutualistic relationships: Badgers can also engage in mutualistic relationships with other species, where both parties benefit. For instance, badgers and foxes may share the same sett, providing one another with additional security and warmth during winter months.

4. Habitat engineers: As badgers dig their setts and forage for food, they can alter the structure and composition of their habitat, creating microhabitats that can benefit other species. The creation of setts can provide shelter and nesting sites for smaller mammals, reptiles, and amphibians. Additionally, badger foraging behaviour can promote soil aeration and nutrient cycling, contributing to overall ecosystem health.

5. Indirect effects: Badgers can also have indirect effects on other species through trophic cascades or other ecological processes. For example, by preying on agricultural pests, badgers can provide a valuable ecosystem service to farmers, reducing the need for chemical pest control and promoting more sustainable agricultural practices.

Understanding the complex interactions between badgers and other species is essential for the effective management and conservation of badger populations and the ecosystems in which they reside. By maintaining healthy badger populations, we can help ensure the continued functioning and resilience of the ecosystems they inhabit.

VII. Summary and Conclusion

Badgers are an integral part of the ecosystems they inhabit, contributing to the maintenance of ecological balance and functioning through their interactions with other species. Their distribution spans a wide range of habitats across Europe, reflecting their adaptability and resilience to various environmental conditions. Despite this adaptability, badger populations are susceptible to human-induced range changes, habitat loss and fragmentation, persecution, and climate change impacts.

Understanding the complex relationships between badgers and their habitat, as well as their interactions with other species, is crucial for the development and implementation of effective conservation strategies. By studying and conserving badger populations, we can contribute to the protection and preservation of the ecosystems they inhabit, ensuring their continued health and resilience for future generations.

In conclusion, badgers play a significant role in the ecosystems they occupy and have a diverse range of interactions with other species. Conservation efforts must consider the various factors influencing badger distribution and habitat, as well as their ecological relationships, in order to develop comprehensive and effective strategies for their protection and long-term survival.

Chapter IX: Threats and Conservation

(© J. McGarrity)

I. Brief Introduction

Badgers, iconic and fascinating creatures, play a vital role in maintaining the balance of their ecosystems. However, these animals face various threats, such as habitat loss, climate change, and human activities, that jeopardise their survival. This chapter delves into the challenges and opportunities in badger conservation, discussing the complexity of conservation issues and the importance of interdisciplinary approaches. We will explore the effectiveness of current conservation strategies, examining their successes and limitations while identifying areas for improvement and future directions. Additionally, we will consider a range of threats, including pollution, pesticides, invasive species, illegal wildlife trade, hybridisation, and issues related to population genetics and inbreeding. By understanding these challenges, we can work towards ensuring the long-term survival of badger populations and preserving the rich biodiversity of their habitats.

II. Challenges and Opportunities in Badger Conservation

A. Complexity of conservation issues: Badger conservation involves a multitude of interconnected factors, such as habitat management, human-wildlife conflicts, and the influence of diseases and invasive species. This section will explore the intricacies of these issues and how they impact badger populations.

B. Balancing human interests and wildlife conservation: As human populations expand and land use changes, conflicts between human interests and badger conservation may arise. This section will discuss the challenges in finding a balance between economic development, agriculture, and conservation efforts while ensuring the well-being of both badgers and humans.

C. Importance of interdisciplinary approaches: To tackle the complex issues surrounding badger conservation, collaborative efforts that combine expertise from various fields, such as ecology, social sciences, and economics, are crucial. This section will highlight the significance of interdisciplinary approaches in addressing conservation challenges and implementing effective solutions.

III. Effectiveness of Current Conservation Strategies

A. Successes and limitations: This section will evaluate the effectiveness of existing conservation strategies for badgers, highlighting their achievements and identifying areas where these strategies may fall short.

B. Areas for improvement and future directions: Building on the discussion of the successes and limitations of current strategies, this section will explore opportunities for enhancement and suggest potential future directions for badger conservation efforts. This may include new approaches, technologies, and collaborations to address ongoing and emerging challenges.

IV. Pollution and Pesticides

A. Impacts on badgers and their ecosystems: This section will discuss the various ways pollution and pesticides can negatively affect badgers and the ecosystems in which they live. This will include direct effects on badger health, as well as indirect consequences through changes to their habitats and food sources.

B. Strategies for mitigation: In response to the harmful effects of pollution and pesticides, this section will present strategies to mitigate these impacts on badgers and their ecosystems. This may involve changes in agricultural practices, regulations, and increased awareness of the issue.

V. Invasive Species

A. Impacts on badgers and their ecosystems: This section will discuss the ways invasive species can adversely affect badgers and their ecosystems. This will include competition for resources, predation, and the introduction of new diseases or parasites.

B. Control and management strategies: In response to the challenges posed by invasive species, this section will present various strategies for controlling and managing them to minimise their impact on badgers and their ecosystems. This may involve habitat restoration, biological control methods, and targeted removal of invasive species.

VI. Illegal Wildlife Trade

A. Impacts on badger populations: This section will examine the ways illegal wildlife trade can negatively affect badger populations, including the capture and sale of live badgers for the pet trade, hunting for fur or traditional medicine, and the secondary impacts on badger habitats.

B. Combating illegal trade: In response to the challenges posed by illegal wildlife trade, this section will outline various strategies and measures that can be implemented to address the issue. These may include stronger law enforcement, public awareness campaigns, and international collaboration to shut down illegal trade routes and networks.

VII. Hybridization

A. Genetic consequences for badger populations: This section will discuss the potential impacts of hybridization between badger species, including the potential for genetic introgression, loss of local adaptations, and reduced genetic diversity.

B. Management and prevention: To address the potential issues caused by hybridization, this section will describe various management strategies and preventative measures that can be employed, such as monitoring and controlling the movement of individuals between populations, genetic assessments, and maintaining habitat barriers that prevent interbreeding between different badger species.

VIII. Population Genetics and Inbreeding

A. Effects on badger population health and resilience: This section will cover the consequences of inbreeding within badger populations, such as reduced genetic diversity, increased vulnerability to diseases and pathogens, and lowered overall population resilience.

B. Strategies for maintaining genetic diversity: In order to address the challenges posed by inbreeding, this section will discuss various strategies that can be implemented to promote genetic diversity, including habitat restoration and connectivity, translocation programs, and the importance of preserving large, genetically diverse populations.

IX. Summary and Conclusion

In conclusion, this chapter has examined various challenges and opportunities in badger conservation, including the effectiveness of current conservation strategies, pollution and pesticides, invasive species, illegal wildlife trade, hybridisation, and population genetics and inbreeding. Each section highlighted the specific issues faced by badgers and their ecosystems, as well as potential solutions and future directions for research and management.

By understanding these complex issues, stakeholders can work together to develop and implement effective conservation strategies, ensuring the long-term survival and wellbeing of badger populations. It is crucial that interdisciplinary approaches are adopted, and that international cooperation is fostered to promote a sustainable future for badgers and the ecosystems in which they live.

Chapter V: Diet and Foraging Behaviour

(Seen at the British Wildlife Centre, Newchapel, Surrey. © Peter Trimming.)

I. Introduction

Badgers, as opportunistic omnivores, have a varied diet that allows them to adapt to different environments and food availability. Their foraging behaviour is influenced by factors such as habitat, season, and the presence of other predators. In this chapter, we will explore the diverse food sources that badgers rely on, their nutritional requirements, and how their diet changes with seasonal variations. Additionally, we will discuss the foraging strategies employed by badgers and their interactions with other predators in terms of competition, predation, mutualism, and niche partitioning. Finally, we will examine the implications of human-badger interactions on diet and foraging and potential conservation efforts to minimise conflicts arising from these interactions.

II. Food Sources

Badgers are known for their diverse and adaptable diet, which comprises a wide range of food sources. These food sources can be broadly categorised as follows:

1. Invertebrates: A significant portion of a badger's diet consists of invertebrates such as earthworms, insects (including beetles, larvae, and ants), and snails. Earthworms, in particular, are a staple food source for badgers in many regions, providing them with essential nutrients.

2. Small mammals: Badgers also prey on small mammals like mice, voles, and shrews. These mammals serve as important sources of protein and energy for badgers, especially during seasons when other food sources are scarce.

3. Birds and eggs: Although not a primary food source, badgers occasionally consume birds, particularly ground-nesting species, as well as their eggs. This opportunistic behaviour enables badgers to make the most of available resources in their environment.

4. Amphibians and reptiles: Badgers may also feed on amphibians such as frogs and toads, as well as reptiles such as lizards and snakes. While these are less common food sources, they contribute to the badger's diverse diet.

5. Fruits and seeds: In the autumn months, badgers supplement their diet with fruits and seeds. This includes berries, apples, and other fruits found in their habitat. Consuming fruits and seeds provides badgers with additional carbohydrates, vitamins, and minerals, which are essential for their overall health.

6. Carrion: Badgers are known to scavenge on carrion, particularly during times when other food sources are scarce. This behaviour not only provides them with essential nutrients but also aids in the decomposition of dead animals in their environment.

The variety of food sources available to badgers allows them to adapt to changing environmental conditions and ensures they can meet their nutritional requirements throughout the year.

III. Nutritional Requirements

Badgers, like all animals, require a balanced diet to maintain their overall health and meet their energy needs. Their nutritional requirements consist of the following essential components:

1. Proteins: Proteins are essential for growth, tissue repair, and immune function. Badgers obtain most of their protein from animal sources such as invertebrates, small mammals, and occasionally birds and amphibians.

2. Fats: Fats are a vital energy source for badgers, especially during the winter months when food is scarce. Fats aid badgers in maintaining their body temperature, and they store excess fat in their bodies for times when food is less abundant.

3. Carbohydrates: Although badgers primarily consume animal matter, they also rely on carbohydrates found in fruits and seeds to meet their energy needs. Carbohydrates offer an important source of energy, especially during the autumn months when fruits are abundant.

4. Vitamins: Vitamins are essential for maintaining various bodily functions, such as immune function, vision, and metabolism. Badgers acquire vitamins from their varied diet, including fruits, seeds, and animal matter.

5. Minerals: Minerals are vital for maintaining strong bones, muscle function, and nerve function. Badgers obtain minerals from a variety of food sources, including invertebrates, small mammals, and fruits.

6. Water: Water is a crucial component of any diet and is necessary for the proper functioning of cells, tissues, and organs. Badgers obtain water from their food and also drink from natural sources such as streams and puddles.

(© Unknown)

By consuming a diverse range of food sources, badgers can meet their nutritional requirements throughout the year. This adaptability allows them to thrive in a variety of habitats and changing environmental conditions.

(© Unknown)

IV. Seasonal Variation in Diet

Badgers' diet varies throughout the year, reflecting the changing availability of food resources in different seasons. This adaptability enables badgers to thrive in various habitats and cope with fluctuating environmental conditions.

1. Spring: In spring, badgers take advantage of the increased availability of invertebrates such as earthworms, beetles, and slugs. These prey items become more abundant owing to the warmer, wetter conditions. Badgers may also consume amphibians, such as frogs and newts, which are active during this period.

2. Summer: During the summer months, badgers continue to feed on invertebrates and small mammals. However, they also diversify their diet to include seasonal fruits, such as berries and cherries, which are rich in carbohydrates and provide a valuable energy source. Birds and their eggs may also be targeted during this time when nests are active.

3. Autumn: As the season transitions to autumn, badgers focus more on foraging for fruits and seeds, which are abundant during this period. Acorns, nuts, and various berries supply carbohydrates and fats that are essential for building up energy reserves in preparation for the winter months. Invertebrates and small mammals remain part of their diet but may be less abundant as temperatures cool.

4. Winter: During the winter months, badgers rely heavily on their fat reserves to meet their energy needs. As food sources become scarcer, badgers may venture out to forage for any remaining invertebrates, small mammals, or carrion. They may also consume roots and tubers when other food sources are scarce.

The seasonal variation in badgers' diets demonstrates their adaptability and ability to thrive in different environments. By adjusting their food consumption to match seasonal food availability, badgers can maintain their energy needs and ensure their survival throughout the year.

VI. Interaction with Other Predators

(© Unknown)

Badgers coexist with various other predators in their habitats, resulting in diverse interactions, such as competition, predation, mutualism, and niche partitioning.

1. Competition: Badgers may compete with other predators, including foxes, birds of prey, and other mustelids, for the same food resources, especially when there is a scarcity of prey. This competition can result in aggressive encounters, particularly around shared food sources, as each species tries to secure sufficient resources to meet their nutritional needs.

2. Predation: While badgers are generally not primary targets for large predators due to their size and powerful build, they may occasionally fall prey to larger animals such as eagles, lynxes, or large owls. Badger cubs are more vulnerable and might be targeted by predators like foxes, large birds of prey, or even other badgers during territorial disputes.

3. Mutualism: Some interactions between badgers and other predators can be mutually beneficial. For example, badgers might forage alongside other species, like foxes or birds, taking advantage of disturbances created by the other animals to catch their prey. In return, these animals can benefit from badgers' powerful digging abilities, which can unearth hidden prey.

(© Unknown)

4. Niche partitioning: To minimise competition for resources, badgers and other predators may partition their ecological niches, either by utilising different food sources or by foraging at different times. This allows multiple predator species to coexist within the same habitat, ensuring the availability of resources for all species involved.

In conclusion, badgers interact with other predators in various ways, ranging from competition to mutualism. By adjusting their behaviour and foraging strategies, badgers can coexist with other predator species in the same habitat and contribute to the overall ecological balance.

VII. Human-Badger Interactions in Diet and Foraging

Human-badger interactions in diet and foraging can be complex, as badgers might be drawn to human settlements or agricultural areas in search of food. This can result in conflicts, as well as opportunities for conservation efforts.

1. Conflicts: Badgers may prey on domestic animals such as poultry, rabbits, or lambs, which can lead to conflicts with farmers and property owners. Additionally, badgers may raid crops, particularly those containing fruits or vegetables, causing damage and economic losses for farmers. These conflicts might contribute to negative perceptions of badgers and may result in the persecution of the species.

2. Opportunities for conservation efforts: To minimise conflicts between badgers and humans, various conservation efforts can be implemented. These might include the installation of badger-proof fencing around gardens, farms, and other sensitive areas, or providing alternative food sources, such as supplementary feeding stations, to reduce badger predation on domestic animals and crops. Educational and outreach programmes can also be developed to increase public awareness of badgers' ecological roles and to promote coexistence between badgers and human communities.

In conclusion, human-badger interactions in diet and foraging can be a source of conflict, but they also provide opportunities for conservation efforts aimed at promoting coexistence. By understanding and addressing the factors that drive these interactions, it is possible to minimise negative impacts on both badgers and human communities while ensuring the long-term survival of this unique species.

VIII. Summary and Conclusion

Badgers exhibit a diverse and adaptable diet, which includes invertebrates, small mammals, birds and eggs, amphibians and reptiles, fruits and seeds, and carrion. Their nutritional needs vary based on factors such as life stage and season, leading to a dynamic foraging strategy that enables them to thrive in various habitats.

Badgers' diet can exhibit seasonal variation, reflecting the availability of different food sources throughout the year. Badgers interact with other predators in their ecosystems through competition, predation, mutualism, and niche partitioning. These interactions might be complex, but they ultimately contribute to the overall balance of their environment.

Human-badger interactions concerning diet and foraging can result in conflicts, particularly when badgers prey on domestic animals or raid crops. Nonetheless, these interactions also offer opportunities for conservation efforts, such as badger-proof fencing, supplementary feeding stations, and educational outreach programmes, aimed at fostering coexistence between badgers and humans.

In conclusion, understanding the diet and foraging behaviour of badgers is crucial for their conservation and the maintenance of healthy ecosystems. By taking into account their diverse food sources, nutritional requirements, and interactions with other species, it is possible to develop effective strategies that ensure the long-term survival of badgers while promoting harmony between these remarkable animals and human communities.

Chapter VI: Social Structure and Behaviour

(© By H. Zell)

I. Introduction

Badgers, belonging to the family Mustelidae, display a range of fascinating social structures and behaviours that have intrigued researchers for decades. The complexity of their social interactions and the adaptability of their behaviours to various environmental conditions have made badgers an important subject of study for understanding the ecological and evolutionary dynamics of group living in mammals. This chapter aims to provide an overview of the social structure and behaviours exhibited by badgers, discussing the advantages and drawbacks of group living, clan organization, social hierarchy, group size dynamics, territoriality, group cohesion, communication, play behaviour, and interspecific interactions. Additionally, this chapter will address the various ways in which badgers interact with humans, as well as the implications these interactions have on their behaviour and social structure.

II. Advantages and Drawbacks of Group Living

Badgers exhibit a range of social structures, from solitary to group living, depending on various factors such as resource availability, population density, and habitat type. Both solitary and group living have their respective benefits and drawbacks, which are explored below.

A. Advantages of Group Living:

1. Enhanced protection: Living in groups can provide increased protection from predators, as a larger number of individuals can detect threats more efficiently and deter potential attacks.

2. Resource sharing: Group living allows for the sharing of resources such as food, shelter, and information, which can improve individual fitness and survival.

3. Social learning: Living in groups enables the transfer of knowledge and skills among individuals, which can be vital for the development and success of young animals.

4. Cooperative behaviour: Group living facilitates cooperative behaviours such as cooperative foraging, denning, defence, and alloparental care, which can increase the overall success of the group.

B. Drawbacks of Group Living:

1. Increased competition: Living in groups can lead to greater competition for limited resources such as food, mates, and shelter, which may negatively impact individual fitness.

2. Disease transmission: The close proximity of individuals in a group can facilitate the spread of diseases and parasites, posing a risk to the overall health of the group.

3. Reproductive suppression: In some group-living species, dominant individuals may suppress the reproduction of subordinates, leading to reduced genetic diversity and potential inbreeding.

While group living offers several advantages, it also comes with its share of challenges. Badgers, like many other social creatures, must navigate these trade-offs to maximise their survival and reproductive success in their respective habitats.

III. Clan Organization and Social Hierarchy

European badgers (Meles meles) exhibit a complex social structure, often living in groups known as clans. These clans exhibit a distinct organisation and hierarchy, which play a crucial role in the maintenance of social bonds and the efficient use of resources within the group.

A. Clan Composition:

1. Clan size: Clan sizes can vary widely depending on factors such as habitat quality, resource availability, and population density. Clans typically comprise 4-12 individuals but can reach up to 20 or more members in some cases.

2. Setts: Badgers live in underground burrows known as setts, which can be extensive and shared by multiple individuals within the clan. Setts provide shelter, protection, and a space for breeding and raising young.

B. Social Hierarchy:

1. Dominant breeding pair: A dominant male and female typically lead the clan, with the pair often having priority access to resources and mating opportunities.

2. Subordinate adults: Subordinate adults are those individuals who do not hold a dominant position within the group. They may be related or unrelated to the dominant pair and may have limited mating opportunities.

3. Juveniles and cubs: Young badgers are born in the sett and rely on the care and protection of the clan members, particularly their mother and other adult females.

C. Factors Influencing Hierarchy: Several factors can influence the formation and maintenance of the social hierarchy, including age, size, sex, and reproductive status. The hierarchy can also be influenced by the quality and availability of resources within the clan's territory.

D. Hierarchy Maintenance: The social hierarchy is maintained through a variety of behaviours, including ritualised aggression, submission signals, social grooming and bonding, and spatial avoidance. These behaviours help to minimise conflicts within the group and maintain social cohesion.

Understanding badger clan organisation and social hierarchy is essential for studying their behaviour, ecology, and conservation. These complex social structures contribute to their ability to adapt and thrive in a wide range of habitats across their distribution range.

IV. Group Size Dynamics

The size of badger clans can vary greatly, influenced by a range of factors that determine the optimal balance between the benefits and costs of group living. Understanding the dynamics of group size is crucial for comprehending the complex social structure and behaviour of badgers.

A. Factors Affecting Group Size:

1. Habitat quality: The quality of a badger's habitat, including the availability of food, shelter, and water, can significantly impact the size of a clan. In areas with abundant resources, badger clans tend to be larger.

2. Resource availability: The distribution and abundance of food sources can play a vital role in determining group size. Clans tend to be larger in areas with plentiful, stable food supplies.

3. Population density: Local badger population density can influence group size, with higher population densities often leading to larger clans as they compete for resources.

B. Dynamics of Group Size:

1. Seasonal variation: The size of badger clans can fluctuate throughout the year due to changes in resource availability, reproductive behaviour, and mortality rates.

2. Dispersal: Young badgers may leave their natal clan in search of new territories and mating opportunities, affecting both the size of the original clan and the formation of new groups.

3. Immigration and emigration: The movement of individuals between clans can impact group size, particularly when new individuals join existing groups or when members leave to form new clans.

The group size dynamics of badger clans play a significant role in their ecology, social structure, and behaviour. These factors are essential for understanding the adaptability and resilience of badgers in changing environments, as well as informing effective conservation strategies.

VI. Group Cohesion and Social Bonds

Maintaining group cohesion and strong social bonds is essential for the success of badger clans, as it enables them to effectively navigate the challenges of their habitat, access resources, and ensure the survival of their offspring. Various behaviours contribute to the development and maintenance of these social bonds.

A. Cooperation:

1. Cooperative foraging: Badgers within a clan often work together to locate and access food resources, increasing their efficiency and overall success.

2. Cooperative denning: Clan members cooperate in the construction, maintenance, and defence of their setts, creating a safe and secure environment for all members of the group.

3. Cooperative defence: Badgers in a clan will band together to defend their territory and sett from potential threats, such as predators or rival badgers.

B. Alloparental care:

1. Cooperative babysitting: Non-breeding adults within the clan may help care for and protect the young, ensuring their safety and increasing their chances of survival.

2. Food provisioning: Alloparents may assist in providing food for the offspring, increasing the overall resources available to the young and contributing to their growth and development.

C. Social bonds and stress reduction:

1. Social grooming: Badgers engage in grooming behaviours to strengthen social bonds within the clan and reduce stress levels among individuals.

2. Play behaviour: Playful interactions among badgers, particularly among juveniles, help to establish and maintain social bonds, develop social skills, and reduce stress.

D. Conflict management:

1. Dominance hierarchy: A clear hierarchy within the clan helps to minimise conflicts and maintain group stability.

2. Ritualised aggression: Displays of aggression can help to manage conflicts without causing physical harm, allowing for the maintenance of social bonds and cohesion.

The cohesion and social bonds within badger clans play a crucial role in their success, survival, and overall well-being. Understanding these aspects of badger social structure provides valuable insights into their ecology, behaviour, and adaptability in the face of changing habitats.

VII. Play Behaviour and Social Learning

(© Unknown)

Play behaviour is a crucial aspect of badger social life, particularly for juveniles. Engaging in play allows badgers to develop their social skills, strengthen bonds within the clan, and learn important behaviours necessary for survival in their environment. Additionally, play behaviour contributes to overall physical development, cognitive skills, and emotional well-being.

A. Types of play behaviour:

1. Play fighting: Badgers often engage in mock battles, which help them develop their physical strength, coordination, and agility. This also allows them to practice defensive and aggressive tactics they may need in future encounters with other animals.

2. Object play: Badgers, especially juveniles, may manipulate objects such as sticks, leaves, or stones, which can help develop their problem-solving skills and dexterity.

3. Social play: Badgers engage in various forms of social play, such as chasing, wrestling, and grooming, which helps to establish and maintain social bonds and hierarchy within the clan.

B. Social learning:

1. Observational learning: Young badgers learn by observing the behaviours and actions of their parents and other clan members. This may include foraging techniques, denning, and territorial marking.

2. Imitation: Juvenile badgers often imitate the behaviours of older clan members, which allows them to acquire skills and knowledge necessary for survival and social integration.

3. Teaching: In some instances, adult badgers may actively teach younger clan members specific skills or behaviours, such as foraging techniques, through demonstration and encouragement.

Play behaviour and social learning are vital components of badger development, contributing to their physical, cognitive, and emotional growth. Understanding these aspects of badger social life provides a deeper insight into their behaviour, ecology, and ability to adapt to changing environments.

VIII. Interspecific Interactions

Badgers interact with various other species in their habitat, establishing relationships that can be predatory, competitive, commensal, or mutualistic. Understanding these interactions is essential for comprehending badger ecology and their role within their ecosystems.

A. Predators:

1. Badgers have few natural predators, primarily due to their robust body, powerful build, and ability to defend themselves. However, they may be preyed upon by large carnivores such as eagles, lynxes, or large owls.

2. Juvenile badgers are more vulnerable to predation by birds of prey, foxes, or other medium-sized carnivores.

B. Competitors:

1. Badgers may compete with other mustelids, such as otters or martens, for resources like food or den sites.

2. They also compete with other mammal species, such as foxes, for similar food resources, including small mammals, birds, and invertebrates.

C. Commensal relationships:

1. Some species may benefit from badger activities without necessarily affecting the badgers themselves. For example, birds or small mammals may use abandoned badger setts for shelter or nesting.

2. Insect-eating birds may follow badgers during foraging activities to feed on insects disturbed by the badger's digging.

D. Mutualistic relationships:

    1. Badgers may form mutualistic relationships with other species, where both parties benefit. For example, some badger populations have been observed cooperating with coyotes while hunting ground squirrels, increasing the hunting success for both species.

E. Parasites and disease:

    1. Like all mammals, badgers can host various parasites, such as ticks, fleas, or internal parasites like worms.

    2. Badgers can also be affected by diseases, including bovine tuberculosis or canine distemper, which can have significant impacts on their populations and influence their interactions with other species, including humans.

F. Human interactions:

    1. Badgers interact with humans in various ways, including through habitat loss, road casualties, or conflicts arising from badgers preying on domestic animals or raiding crops.

    2. Conservation efforts and awareness campaigns can help mitigate negative human-badger interactions and promote coexistence between the species.

By understanding the different interspecific interactions badgers engage in, we can better appreciate their ecological role and the importance of conserving their populations and habitats.

IX. Human Interactions

Badgers and humans have a complex relationship, characterised by both conflict and coexistence. In order to promote the conservation of badgers and their habitats, it is essential to understand the various ways in which humans and badgers interact.

A. Habitat loss:

    1. Human activities such as urbanisation, agriculture, and deforestation can lead to the loss or degradation of badger habitats, causing population declines and range contractions.

    2. Conservation efforts, including the protection and restoration of badger habitats, can help mitigate the negative impacts of human-induced habitat loss.

B. Road casualties:

(Badger road casualty. © Badenoch and Strathspey Conservation Group)

1. Badgers are frequently victims of road traffic accidents, which can significantly impact local populations.

2. Measures such as wildlife crossings or speed limit reductions in areas known for badger presence can help reduce the number of road casualties.

C. Conflicts with agriculture:

1. Badgers can cause damage to crops, leading to conflicts with farmers.

2. Non-lethal mitigation strategies, such as fencing or deterrents, can help minimise crop damage and foster coexistence between badgers and farmers.

D. Livestock predation:

1. In some instances, badgers may prey on small domestic animals like poultry, leading to conflicts with farmers or rural communities.

2. Protective measures, including secure enclosures for poultry or livestock, can reduce the risk of predation by badgers.

E. Disease transmission:

1. Badgers can act as reservoirs for diseases, such as bovine tuberculosis, which may impact livestock and pose challenges for wildlife management and conservation.

2. Effective disease management strategies, including vaccination programmes and regular monitoring, can help control disease transmission between badgers and livestock.

F. Conservation and public awareness:

1. Raising public awareness about badgers and their ecological importance can help encourage a greater understanding of the species and promote coexistence between badgers and humans.

2. Conservation efforts, such as habitat protection, research, and legal measures, can contribute to the long-term survival of badger populations.

By recognising the various ways in which humans and badgers interact, we can develop strategies to minimise conflicts, promote coexistence, and ensure the conservation of badgers and their habitats.

X. Summary and Conclusion

In summary, the European badger's reproductive life cycle is a complex and fascinating process, which involves a unique mating system, delayed implantation, and varying degrees of parental care. The different stages of reproduction and development, from mate selection and mating rituals to gestation, birth, and cub development, play a crucial role in the survival and success of this species.

Mortality and lifespan are influenced by both natural factors, such as predation, disease, and intra-species competition, and human-induced factors, including road traffic accidents, illegal persecution, and habitat loss. Understanding these factors and their impact on badger populations is vital for their conservation and management.

In conclusion, the study of the European badger's reproductive life cycle and the factors that influence its mortality and lifespan offers valuable insights into the complex social dynamics, ecological interactions, and challenges faced by this species. By addressing human-induced threats and promoting conservation efforts, we can contribute to the long-term survival and well-being of the European badger and the ecosystems in which they live.

Chapter VII: Reproduction and Life Cycle

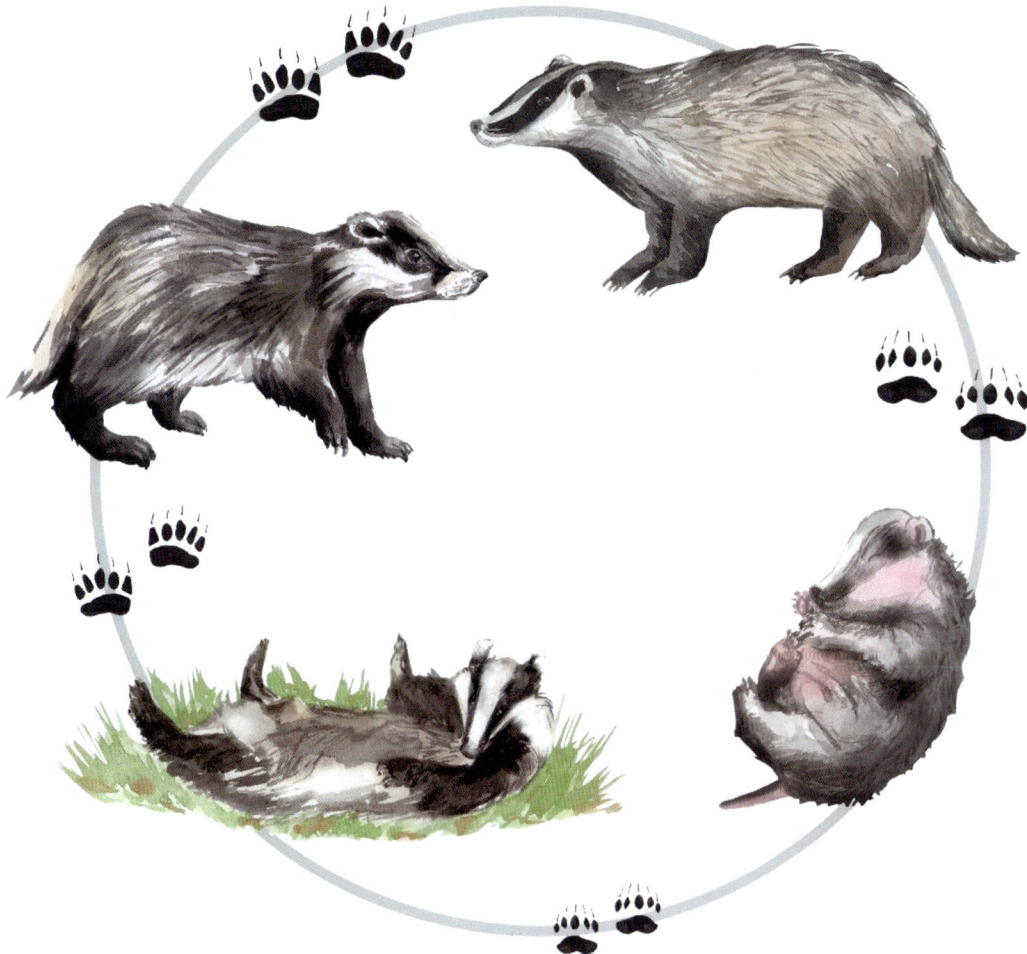

(Badger lifecycle)

I. Introduction

The reproductive process and life cycle of the European badger (Meles meles) are complex and fascinating aspects of its biology. Understanding these aspects is crucial for the conservation and management of this species. In this chapter, we will delve into the mating system and mate selection, mating rituals and copulation, gestation and delayed implantation, birth and litter size, parental care and cub development, as well as the various stages of growth and factors influencing mortality and lifespan. Through this comprehensive examination, we aim to provide a thorough understanding of the reproductive strategies and life cycle of the European badger.

II. Mating System and Mate Selection

The European badger exhibits a predominantly polygamous mating system, with both males and females mating with multiple partners. However, the degree of polygamy can vary depending on the social structure and ecological factors of the population.

Males and females engage in mate selection based on various factors, including social hierarchy, physical condition, age, and experience. Dominant individuals often have priority access to mating opportunities, while subordinate individuals may also mate, but to a lesser extent. Physical condition plays a role in attracting potential mates, with healthy, well-nourished individuals generally being more attractive to the opposite sex.

Scent communication is crucial during the mating season, as it provides information about the reproductive status and condition of potential mates. Both males and females use scent marking to advertise their presence and attract partners. Timing and synchrony are also important, as badgers generally mate during the winter months, with the peak mating period occurring from December to February.

Mate guarding is a common behaviour in badgers, where males attempt to maintain close proximity to receptive females, protecting them from rival males and increasing their chances of successful copulation. Infanticide, while rare, may occur in badger populations as a result of reproductive competition, with males killing the offspring of rival males to increase their own reproductive success.

In summary, the mating system of European badgers is complex, with multiple factors influencing mate selection and mating success. Understanding these factors is essential for a comprehensive understanding of the species' reproductive behaviour and overall life cycle.

III. Mating Rituals and Copulation

The mating rituals of European badgers involve a combination of scent marking, vocalisations, and physical interactions. Scent marking is particularly important in the badger mating process, as it allows individuals to communicate their reproductive status and attract potential mates. Badgers utilise specialised scent glands to deposit their scent on trees, grass, and other objects within their territory.

Vocalisations are another means of communication during the mating season. Males and females emit a variety of calls, including churrs, whickers, and keckers, which serve to attract and engage potential mates. These vocalisations can help in coordinating the mating process and establishing pair bonds.

Physical interactions play a crucial role in the courtship display. Badgers engage in mutual grooming, nuzzling, and play-fighting as part of their mating rituals. These behaviours help to strengthen pair bonds and ensure the receptivity of both partners.

Reproductive competition among males can lead to aggressive encounters, particularly when resources and mates are scarce. Dominant males may assert their social status to secure mating opportunities, while subordinate males may attempt to mate covertly.

Copulation in badgers typically involves the male initiating contact by approaching the female and gently nudging her. If receptive, the female will allow the male to mount her. The mounting process involves the male positioning himself on the female's back, with both animals facing the same direction. Penetration and intromission follow, and a copulatory lock may occur, during which the male's penis swells, securing the pair together. The copulatory lock can last anywhere from a few minutes to over an hour, ensuring successful sperm transfer. Following ejaculation, the male dismounts and may engage in post-copulatory grooming with the female.

Overall, mating rituals and copulation in European badgers are complex processes involving a combination of scent marking, vocalisations, and physical interactions. These behaviours are essential for successful reproduction and the continuation of the species.

IV. Gestation, Delayed Implantation, and Birth

Gestation in European badgers is a unique process, as it involves a period of delayed implantation. After successful copulation and fertilisation, the fertilised egg (zygote) undergoes a few cell divisions before entering a state of dormancy. During this period, the zygote does not implant itself into the uterus, and no further development occurs.

Delayed implantation in badgers can last for several months, typically from autumn until late winter or early spring. This adaptive strategy allows badgers to time the birth of their cubs to coincide with the availability of abundant food resources. Once the conditions are favourable, hormonal changes trigger the implantation of the embryo into the uterine lining, and active gestation begins.

The active gestation period in European badgers lasts for approximately six to eight weeks. During this time, the developing embryos grow rapidly and undergo significant differentiation. At the end of the gestation period, the female gives birth to a litter of cubs.

Litter size in badgers can vary, with an average of two to three cubs born per litter. However, litter sizes can range from one to five cubs, depending on factors such as the female's age, health, and environmental conditions. The cubs are born in a specialised chamber within the sett, which is lined with soft bedding materials like grass and leaves.

New-born badger cubs are altricial, meaning they are born in a relatively undeveloped state. They are blind, hairless, and completely dependent on their mother for care and nourishment. The mother will nurse her cubs for several weeks, providing them with vital nutrients and antibodies to ensure their survival and growth.

In summary, the gestation period in European badgers involves a unique mechanism of delayed implantation, which allows them to time the birth of their cubs to coincide with optimal environmental conditions. After active gestation, the female gives birth to a litter of altricial cubs, which rely on maternal care for survival and development.

(European Badger Cubs © Victoria Hillman)

V. Parental Care and Cub Development

Parental care in European badgers is crucial for the survival and development of their offspring. Both maternal and alloparental care contribute to the well-being and growth of the cubs during their early stages of life.

Maternal care: The mother badger is the primary caregiver for her cubs. She is responsible for nursing, grooming, and protecting her offspring from potential threats. The mother stays close to her cubs in the first few weeks, rarely leaving the sett to ensure their safety. She provides her cubs with milk, which is rich in nutrients and antibodies essential for their growth and immune system development.

Paternal care: While the role of male badgers in parental care is limited compared to the mother, they may still contribute by protecting the territory, maintaining the sett, and participating in social grooming. Some dominant males have been observed to show interest in the cubs and interact with them, though their involvement in direct care is minimal.

Alloparental care: In addition to maternal care, other members of the badger social group can also contribute to the well-being of the cubs. Alloparental care, provided by non-parental adults or older siblings, can involve grooming, playing, and even babysitting. This support system helps to strengthen social bonds within the group and may increase the survival chances of the cubs.

Cub development occurs in several stages:

1. Neonatal stage (0-4 weeks): Cubs are born blind, hairless, and fully dependent on their mother. During this stage, the mother provides milk, warmth, and protection.

2. Early socialisation (4-8 weeks): Cubs' eyes open, and they begin to grow fur. They start to explore their surroundings and interact with their siblings and other members of the social group.

3. Exploration and learning (2-4 months): Cubs venture outside the sett and start learning essential skills such as foraging, grooming, and social interactions.

4. Juvenile stage (4-12 months): Cubs gradually become more independent and start to contribute to the social group's activities, although they still rely on adults for protection and guidance.

5. Adulthood (1 year onwards): Cubs reach sexual maturity and become fully integrated members of the social group, participating in all aspects of group life.

In conclusion, parental care in European badgers plays a vital role in the development and survival of their offspring. Both maternal and alloparental care contribute to the well-being of the cubs, while their development progresses through distinct stages, ultimately leading to their integration into the social group as adults.

VII. Mortality and Lifespan

Mortality and lifespan in European badgers are influenced by various factors, including natural causes and human-induced threats. Understanding these factors is essential for the conservation and management of badger social groups.

Natural factors: Predation, disease, and intra-species competition can all contribute to badger mortality. Young cubs are especially vulnerable to predation by larger carnivores, such as foxes, birds of prey, and even other badgers. Disease, including bovine tuberculosis and various parasites, can also impact badger social groups. Intra-species competition for resources and territory can lead to injuries or even fatalities in severe cases.

Human-induced factors: Human activities have a significant impact on badger mortality rates. Road traffic accidents are a common cause of death for badgers, particularly in areas where roads fragment their habitat. Illegal persecution, including baiting and snaring, also contributes to badger mortality. Additionally, habitat loss and fragmentation due to urbanisation and agricultural intensification can lead to decreased food availability and increased competition, indirectly affecting badger survival rates.

Lifespan: European badgers have a relatively long lifespan for a mustelid species. In the wild, they can live up to 14 years, although the average lifespan is typically between 5 and 8 years. In captivity, with a lack of predators and access to consistent food and medical care, badgers can live up to 15-16 years. However, it is essential to note that a significant proportion of badgers do not survive past their first year of life due to the many challenges they face during this critical period.

In conclusion, mortality and lifespan in European badgers are influenced by a combination of natural and human-induced factors. Efforts to minimise human-induced threats, such as habitat loss, fragmentation, and illegal persecution, can help improve badger survival rates and contribute to the long-term conservation of the species.

VIII. Summary and Conclusion

In summary, the European badger's reproductive life cycle is a complex and fascinating process, which involves a unique mating system, delayed implantation, and varying degrees of parental care. The different stages of reproduction and development, from mate selection and mating rituals to gestation, birth, and cub development, play a crucial role in the survival and success of this species.

Mortality and lifespan are influenced by both natural factors, such as predation, disease, and intra-species competition, and human-induced factors, including road traffic accidents, illegal persecution, and habitat loss. Understanding these factors and their impact on badger social groups is essential for their conservation and management.

In conclusion, the study of the European badger's reproductive life cycle and the factors that influence its mortality and lifespan offers valuable insights into the complex social dynamics, ecological interactions, and challenges faced by this species. By addressing human-induced threats and promoting conservation efforts, we can contribute to the long-term survival and well-being of the European badger and the ecosystems in which they live.

Chapter VIII: Ecology and Conservation

(© J. McGarrity)

I. Introduction

Badgers (Meles meles) are medium-sized mammals belonging to the Mustelidae family, which includes otters, weasels, and ferrets. As native species to Europe and parts of Asia, badgers play crucial roles in maintaining the health and balance of their ecosystems. Understanding the complex interplay of ecology, human activities, and conservation efforts is essential for the preservation of these iconic creatures.

This chapter will provide an overview of the ecology and conservation of badgers, focusing on their roles within ecosystems, the impact of human activities on their populations, and the various conservation measures and initiatives aimed at ensuring their survival. We will also examine the influence of climate change on badger populations and their habitats, as well as the ecological interactions that shape their behaviour and distribution. Finally, we will discuss the importance of badgers as keystone and indicator species and the implications for conservation efforts.

II. Badgers in Ecosystems: Roles and Importance

(Badger sett © Unknown)

Badgers fulfil several essential functions within their ecosystems, making them a vital component of the habitats they inhabit. Some of the key roles' badgers play in ecosystems include:

1. Predation and prey dynamics: As omnivores, badgers consume a variety of food items, including invertebrates, small mammals, birds, eggs, and plant material. By preying on these organisms, badgers help regulate the populations of other species, maintaining a balanced ecosystem.

2. Seed dispersal: Badgers contribute to the dispersal of seeds, particularly from fruits they consume. By carrying seeds away from the parent plant and distributing them throughout their territories, badgers help facilitate plant regeneration and promote biodiversity.

3. Soil aeration: Badgers are known for their digging abilities, creating extensive burrow systems called setts. Their digging activities help aerate the soil, which can enhance soil fertility and create favourable conditions for plant growth.

4. Impact on vegetation: The foraging behaviour of badgers can influence the composition and structure of vegetation, as they dig for food and create setts. This process can result in the creation of patches of bare ground, which can be colonised by pioneer plant species and contribute to habitat diversity.

5. Disease transmission: Badgers can act as reservoirs for various diseases, such as bovine tuberculosis, which can affect other wildlife, livestock, and humans. Understanding badger ecology and behaviour is essential for the development of effective disease control strategies.

6. Keystone species: As a keystone species, badgers have a disproportionally large impact on their ecosystems relative to their abundance. Their various roles, such as predation, seed dispersal, and soil aeration, have cascading effects on other species and ecosystem processes.

7. Trophic cascades: Badgers can influence the structure and dynamics of ecosystems through their effects on the populations of prey species, resulting in trophic cascades. These cascades can have wide-ranging consequences for the overall health and functioning of ecosystems.

8. Competition and mutualistic relationships: Badgers engage in both competitive and mutualistic interactions with other species. Understanding these interactions can provide valuable insights into the ecology and conservation of badgers and their ecosystems.

9. Indicator species: Badgers can act as indicator species, providing valuable information about the overall health of ecosystems. Monitoring badger populations can help detect environmental stressors, evaluate management strategies, and prioritise conservation efforts.

In conclusion, badgers are integral components of the ecosystems they inhabit, fulfilling various roles that contribute to the overall health and balance of their habitats. Preserving badger populations is crucial for maintaining biodiversity and the proper functioning of ecosystems.

III. Human Impacts on Badger Populations

Human activities have significantly impacted badger populations in various ways, both directly and indirectly. Some of the most notable human impacts on badger populations include:

1. Habitat loss and fragmentation: The conversion of natural habitats for agricultural, urban, and industrial purposes has led to the loss and fragmentation of badger habitats. This can result in smaller, isolated populations, making them more vulnerable to local extinction and reducing their genetic diversity.

2. Use of pesticides and its effects: The widespread use of pesticides in agriculture can have detrimental effects on badger populations. These chemicals can reduce the availability of prey species, such as invertebrates, and cause direct harm to badgers through ingestion or exposure to contaminated food sources.

3. Badger culling and disease control: Badger culling has been implemented in some regions as a strategy for controlling bovine tuberculosis, which can be transmitted between badgers and cattle. However, the effectiveness of culling as a disease control measure remains controversial, and alternative strategies, such as vaccination and improved biosecurity, are being explored.

4. Road mortality and mitigation measures: Roads pose a significant threat to badger populations, with many individuals killed in vehicle collisions each year. Strategies to reduce road mortality include wildlife crossings, traffic calming measures, roadside fencing, and habitat restoration to minimise badger movement across roads.

5. Hunting and trapping regulations: In some areas, badgers have been hunted or trapped for various purposes, such as fur or sport. Overexploitation can lead to population declines, and the implementation of appropriate hunting and trapping regulations is essential for ensuring the long-term survival of badger populations.

6. Climate change: Climate change can impact badger populations through shifts in distribution, abundance, and habitat suitability. Changes in temperature and precipitation patterns can affect the availability of food sources and influence badger behaviour, reproduction, and survival.

To ensure the conservation of badger populations, it is crucial to address these human-induced threats through effective management strategies and policy implementation. Developing a better understanding of badger ecology, behaviour, and the impacts of human activities can provide valuable insights for devising sustainable conservation approaches.

IV. Legal Protections and International Conservation Initiatives

The conservation of badger populations is supported by various legal protections and international conservation initiatives aimed at ensuring their long-term survival. These measures include:

1. National regulations: Legal protections for badgers vary by country, with many European nations implementing laws to safeguard these species. These protections may include restrictions on hunting, trapping, and disturbance of their habitats or setts.

2. Hunting and trapping regulations: In regions where badger hunting and trapping are permitted, regulations are often in place to limit the number of animals that can be taken, designate specific hunting seasons, or require specific methods to minimise harm to the species.

3. Habitat protection: Many countries have established protected areas to conserve essential habitats for badgers and other wildlife species. These areas aim to preserve natural ecosystems and reduce habitat loss and fragmentation caused by human activities.

4. International conservation initiatives: Badgers are also protected by various international agreements and initiatives, including:

a. Convention on Biological Diversity (CBD): The CBD aims to conserve biodiversity, promote the sustainable use of natural resources, and ensure the fair and equitable sharing of benefits arising from genetic resources. As a party to this convention, countries are committed to implementing measures to conserve badger populations and their habitats.

b. Convention on the Conservation of European Wildlife and Natural Habitats (Bern Convention): This convention seeks to conserve wild flora and fauna and their natural habitats, with a particular focus on endangered and vulnerable species, including badgers. The Bern Convention promotes cooperation between countries and the development of policies and legislation to achieve its objectives.

c. International Union for Conservation of Nature (IUCN): The IUCN assesses the conservation status of species worldwide and provides guidelines for their management and protection. Depending on the specific badger species, their listing on the IUCN Red List of Threatened Species may vary, which helps inform conservation actions and policies at national and international levels.

5. Habitat restoration and connectivity: Efforts to restore and maintain habitat connectivity are essential for supporting badger populations. These initiatives may involve creating and

maintaining wildlife corridors, identifying critical linkages, protecting land, and enhancing habitats to support the movement and dispersal of badgers across the landscape.

6. Monitoring and adaptive management: Regular monitoring of badger populations is crucial for assessing their conservation status and informing management decisions. This can involve the use of camera traps, track surveys, radio telemetry, population genetics, and citizen science initiatives. Adaptive management strategies can help ensure that conservation efforts are effective and responsive to changing conditions.

In summary, the conservation of badger populations relies on a combination of legal protections, international initiatives, and targeted management actions to address threats and promote their long-term survival. Effective collaboration between governments, conservation organisations, and local communities is crucial to achieving these goals.

V. Habitat Restoration and Connectivity

Habitat restoration and connectivity are vital components of badger conservation efforts, as they help to mitigate the impacts of habitat loss and fragmentation on badger populations. Ensuring the availability of suitable habitats and facilitating the movement of individuals across the landscape can contribute to the long-term survival of badgers. Key aspects of habitat restoration and connectivity include:

1. Creating and maintaining wildlife corridors: Wildlife corridors are essential for connecting fragmented habitats, enabling badgers to move between them safely. These corridors can take various forms, such as hedgerows, woodlands, or riverine habitats, and are crucial for maintaining gene flow and sustaining viable badger populations.

2. Identifying critical linkages: Conservation efforts should focus on identifying and protecting critical linkages between habitats to ensure connectivity for badgers. This may involve mapping and analysing landscape features, badger movements, and habitat quality to pinpoint areas of high conservation priority.

3. Land protection and management: Protecting key habitats and managing them effectively is essential for badger conservation. This can involve the acquisition of land for conservation purposes, working with landowners to establish agreements or easements, and implementing targeted management practices to enhance habitat quality for badgers.

4. Habitat enhancement: Restoring and enhancing habitats can improve their suitability for badgers and other wildlife species. This may include creating setts, planting native vegetation, or restoring degraded habitats, such as woodland or grassland areas.

5. Monitoring and adaptive management: Regular monitoring of badger populations and habitats is necessary to evaluate the effectiveness of restoration and connectivity efforts. Adaptive management strategies can help ensure that conservation actions are responsive to changing conditions, such as shifts in badger distribution or the emergence of new threats.

In conclusion, habitat restoration and connectivity are essential components of badger conservation, helping to ensure the long-term survival of these species in the face of habitat loss and fragmentation. Through a combination of targeted actions and collaboration among stakeholders, it is possible to create and maintain the necessary conditions to support thriving badger populations.

VI. Monitoring, Population Management, and Adaptive Strategies

Effective conservation of badger populations requires a comprehensive approach to monitoring, population management, and the implementation of adaptive strategies. By regularly assessing the status of badger populations and their habitats, conservationists can develop targeted actions to address emerging threats and ensure the long-term survival of these species. Key aspects of monitoring, population management, and adaptive strategies include:

1. Methods for monitoring badger populations: A range of techniques can be employed to monitor badger populations, such as camera traps, track surveys, radio telemetry, population genetics, and citizen science initiatives. These methods can provide valuable information on badger abundance, distribution, and habitat use, enabling informed conservation decisions.

2. Setting clear objectives: Establishing specific, measurable, achievable, relevant, and time-bound (SMART) objectives for badger conservation can help guide monitoring and management efforts. These objectives should be based on the best available scientific information and take into account the ecological, social, and economic context of the conservation area.

3. Developing and implementing management actions: Based on the monitoring results and established objectives, targeted management actions can be developed to address identified threats and enhance badger populations. These actions may include habitat restoration, the implementation of mitigation measures, or the control of invasive species.

4. Monitoring and evaluation: Regular monitoring of badger populations and habitats is essential for evaluating the effectiveness of conservation actions and informing future management decisions. This may involve tracking changes in badger abundance, distribution, or habitat quality, as well as assessing the impact of implemented actions on badger populations.

5. Adjusting strategies: Adaptive management involves the continuous assessment and adjustment of conservation strategies based on new information and changing circumstances. By remaining flexible and responsive to emerging threats or knowledge, conservationists can improve the overall effectiveness of their efforts to protect badger populations.

In summary, a robust approach to monitoring, population management, and adaptive strategies is essential for ensuring the long-term conservation of badger populations. By regularly assessing the status of badgers and their habitats, and adjusting conservation actions accordingly, it is possible to address emerging threats and maintain the ecological balance necessary for the survival of these species.

VII. Climate Change Impacts on Badgers and Their Habitats

Climate change poses significant challenges for the conservation of badgers and their habitats. As global temperatures rise and weather patterns become more unpredictable, badgers may experience shifts in their distribution and abundance, as well as alterations to the ecosystems in which they live. Key climate change impacts on badgers and their habitats include:

1. Shifts in distribution and abundance: Changes in temperature, precipitation, and the availability of resources may force badgers to move to new areas or alter their behaviours in order to survive. This could result in shifts in their geographic range, local extinctions, or changes in population densities.

2. Adaptation and resilience: Badgers may be able to adapt to some of the impacts of climate change, such as alterations to their habitat or food sources, by adjusting their behaviours or utilising different resources. However, the speed and extent of these adaptations will depend on the species' intrinsic resilience and the magnitude of the changes they face.

3. Changes in ecosystem dynamics: Climate change can lead to alterations in the structure and function of ecosystems, with potential knock-on effects for badgers and other species. For example, changes in plant communities may affect the availability of prey, while alterations to predator-prey dynamics could influence badger survival rates.

4. Increased frequency of extreme weather events: Climate change may result in more frequent and severe storms, floods, droughts, and heatwaves, which can negatively impact badger populations by causing direct mortality or damaging their habitats.

5. Disease transmission: Climate change may influence the distribution and prevalence of diseases affecting badgers, such as bovine tuberculosis, by altering the conditions in which pathogens and their vectors can survive and reproduce. This could lead to increased disease transmission and the emergence of new health threats for badger populations.

In order to safeguard badgers and their habitats in the face of climate change, it is essential that conservation efforts take into account these potential impacts and develop strategies for enhancing the resilience of badger populations. This may involve habitat restoration, the creation of wildlife corridors, and the development of adaptive management strategies that can respond to changing environmental conditions. By taking a proactive and flexible approach to conservation, it is possible to mitigate the adverse effects of climate change and ensure the long-term survival of badgers and their ecosystems.

VIII. Badgers as Keystone and Indicator Species

Badgers play significant roles in their ecosystems, acting as both keystone and indicator species. Understanding these roles can help inform conservation efforts and highlight the importance of protecting badger populations.

1. Keystone species: Badgers are considered keystone species due to their influence on ecosystem structure and function. As predators, they help regulate the populations of their prey, such as small mammals and invertebrates. Additionally, as ecosystem engineers, badgers contribute to soil aeration and nutrient cycling by digging extensive burrow systems (setts). Their activities can also create microhabitats for other species, fostering biodiversity.

2. Influence on trophic cascades: Badgers can indirectly influence the abundance of other species in their ecosystems through trophic cascades. For example, by preying on rodents, badgers can help control the populations of species that feed on vegetation, thereby promoting plant diversity and overall ecosystem health.

3. Implications for conservation: Recognising badgers as keystone species highlights the importance of their conservation. Protecting badger populations can have positive knock-on effects for the overall health and stability of their ecosystems, benefiting a wide range of other species.

4. Indicator species: Badgers can serve as indicator species, reflecting the overall health and stability of their ecosystems. As badgers are sensitive to changes in habitat quality, population densities, and resource availability, monitoring their populations can provide valuable information about the condition of their habitats and the success of conservation efforts.

5. Implications for conservation monitoring: Using badgers as indicator species can help inform conservation efforts in several ways:

a. Early detection of environmental stress: Monitoring badger populations can provide an early warning of environmental problems, such as habitat degradation, pollution, or the spread of disease.

b. Evaluation of management strategies: Tracking badger population trends can help assess the effectiveness of conservation measures, such as habitat restoration or disease control programmes.

c. Prioritisation of conservation efforts: Identifying areas where badger populations are thriving or declining can help focus conservation resources on the most critical habitats and issues.

In summary, understanding the roles of badgers as keystone and indicator species can provide valuable insights for conservation efforts. By monitoring and protecting badger populations, it is possible to contribute to the overall health and resilience of their ecosystems, benefiting a diverse range of species and habitats.

IX. Ecological Interactions

Badgers are an integral part of their ecosystems, interacting with various species in numerous ways. By examining these ecological interactions, we can gain a deeper understanding of badger ecology and the importance of their conservation.

1. Predation and prey dynamics: As opportunistic predators, badgers feed on a variety of prey, including small mammals, invertebrates, birds, and amphibians. By preying on these species, badgers help regulate their populations, maintaining a balance within the ecosystem. Conversely, badgers also face predation from larger carnivores, such as foxes and birds of prey, adding another layer of complexity to the ecological network.

2. Competition: Badgers may engage in both interspecific (between species) and intraspecific (within species) competition for resources, such as food, shelter, and mates. This competition can influence badger populations, social structure, and behaviour, as well as have implications for other species in the ecosystem.

3. Mutualistic relationships: Badgers may participate in indirect mutualistic relationships, benefiting other species through their actions as ecosystem engineers. By digging setts and foraging, badgers can create microhabitats for other species, promote plant growth and diversity, and contribute to soil aeration and nutrient cycling.

4. Seed dispersal: Badgers can play a role in seed dispersal by consuming fruits and seeds, and subsequently depositing them in their faeces. This process helps distribute plant species across the landscape, supporting plant diversity and habitat connectivity.

5. Soil aeration and impact on vegetation: The digging activities of badgers contribute to soil aeration, improving soil quality and promoting the growth of vegetation. This can, in turn, provide habitat and food resources for other species, enhancing overall ecosystem health.

6. Disease transmission: Badgers can act as reservoirs for various diseases, such as bovine tuberculosis, which can have implications for both wildlife and livestock populations. Understanding the dynamics of disease transmission is crucial for informing effective disease management and conservation strategies.

By examining the ecological interactions involving badgers, we can better appreciate their importance within their ecosystems and the broader implications of their conservation. These interactions highlight the interconnectedness of species and the need for holistic approaches to wildlife management and habitat protection.

VIII. Summary and Conclusion

Badgers play a significant role in their ecosystems, participating in various ecological interactions and serving as keystone and indicator species. Their presence and activities contribute to ecosystem health and resilience by regulating prey populations, dispersing seeds, promoting soil aeration and vegetation growth, and forming mutualistic relationships with other species. However, human-induced threats such as habitat loss, road mortality, and badger culling pose challenges to badger populations and their conservation.

Efforts to protect and conserve badgers require a multifaceted approach, including legal protections, international conservation initiatives, habitat restoration and connectivity measures, monitoring and adaptive population management strategies, and public awareness and education. Addressing the impacts of climate change on badger populations and their habitats is also crucial in ensuring the long-term survival of this species.

By understanding the complex ecological interactions involving badgers and the importance of their conservation, we can better inform effective management and conservation strategies. This holistic approach will not only help safeguard badger populations but also contribute to the overall health and resilience of the ecosystems they inhabit.

Chapter X: Conservation Strategies

(© J. McGarrity)

I. Brief Introduction

Badgers, iconic and fascinating creatures, play a vital role in maintaining the balance of their ecosystems. However, these animals face various threats, such as habitat loss, climate change, and human activities, that jeopardise their survival. This chapter delves into the challenges and opportunities in badger conservation, discussing the complexity of conservation issues and the importance of interdisciplinary approaches. We will explore the effectiveness of current conservation strategies, examining their successes and limitations while identifying areas for improvement and future directions. Additionally, we will consider a range of threats, including pollution, pesticides, invasive species, illegal wildlife trade, hybridisation, and issues related to population genetics and inbreeding. By understanding these challenges, we can work towards ensuring the long-term survival of badger populations and preserving the rich biodiversity of their habitats.

II. Challenges and Opportunities in Badger Conservation

A. Complexity of conservation issues: Badger conservation involves a multitude of interconnected factors, such as habitat management, human-wildlife conflicts, and the influence of diseases and invasive species. This section will explore the intricacies of these issues and how they impact badger populations.

B. Balancing human interests and wildlife conservation: As human populations expand and land use changes, conflicts between human interests and badger conservation may arise. This section will discuss the challenges in finding a balance between economic development, agriculture, and conservation efforts while ensuring the well-being of both badgers and humans.

C. Importance of interdisciplinary approaches: To tackle the complex issues surrounding badger conservation, collaborative efforts that combine expertise from various fields, such as ecology, social sciences, and economics, are crucial. This section will highlight the significance of interdisciplinary approaches in addressing conservation challenges and implementing effective solutions.

III. Effectiveness of Current Conservation Strategies

A. Successes and limitations: This section will evaluate the effectiveness of existing conservation strategies for badgers, highlighting their achievements and identifying areas where these strategies may fall short.

B. Areas for improvement and future directions: Building on the discussion of the successes and limitations of current strategies, this section will explore opportunities for enhancement and suggest potential future directions for badger conservation efforts. This may include new approaches, technologies, and collaborations to address ongoing and emerging challenges.

IV. Pollution and Pesticides

A. Impacts on badgers and their ecosystems: This section will discuss the various ways pollution and pesticides can negatively affect badgers and the ecosystems in which they live. This will include direct effects on badger health, as well as indirect consequences through changes to their habitats and food sources.

B. Strategies for mitigation: In response to the harmful effects of pollution and pesticides, this section will present strategies to mitigate these impacts on badgers and their ecosystems. This may involve changes in agricultural practices, regulations, and increased awareness of the issue.

V. Invasive Species

A. Impacts on badgers and their ecosystems: This section will discuss the ways invasive species can adversely affect badgers and their ecosystems. This will include competition for resources, predation, and the introduction of new diseases or parasites.

B. Control and management strategies: In response to the challenges posed by invasive species, this section will present various strategies for controlling and managing them to minimise their impact on badgers and their ecosystems. This may involve habitat restoration, biological control methods, and targeted removal of invasive species.

VI. Illegal Wildlife Trade

A. Impacts on badger populations: This section will examine the ways illegal wildlife trade can negatively affect badger populations, including the capture and sale of live badgers for the pet trade, hunting for fur or traditional medicine, and the secondary impacts on badger habitats.

B. Combating illegal trade: In response to the challenges posed by illegal wildlife trade, this section will outline various strategies and measures that can be implemented to address the issue. These may include stronger law enforcement, public awareness campaigns, and international collaboration to shut down illegal trade routes and networks.

VII. Hybridization

A. Genetic consequences for badger populations: This section will discuss the potential impacts of hybridization between badger species, including the potential for genetic introgression, loss of local adaptations, and reduced genetic diversity.

B. Management and prevention: To address the potential issues caused by hybridization, this section will describe various management strategies and preventative measures that can be employed, such as monitoring and controlling the movement of individuals between populations, genetic assessments, and maintaining habitat barriers that prevent interbreeding between different badger species.

VIII. Population Genetics and Inbreeding

A. Effects on badger population health and resilience: This section will cover the consequences of inbreeding within badger populations, such as reduced genetic diversity, increased vulnerability to diseases and pathogens, and lowered overall population resilience.

B. Strategies for maintaining genetic diversity: In order to address the challenges posed by inbreeding, this section will discuss various strategies that can be implemented to promote genetic diversity, including habitat restoration and connectivity, translocation programmes, and the importance of preserving large, genetically diverse populations.

IX. Summary and Conclusion

This chapter has provided an in-depth exploration of the various conservation strategies implemented to protect badger populations. The discussion began with an overview of the legal protection and regulations in place, both nationally and internationally, to safeguard badgers and their habitats. We then examined habitat restoration and management initiatives, which aim to improve the quality and connectivity of badger habitats, while balancing human development needs.

Human-related threats, such as road casualties, were also addressed, with a focus on mitigation measures to reduce mortality and promote connectivity. The importance of population monitoring and research for informing management strategies was highlighted, followed by an analysis of disease management and control efforts to mitigate risks and promote population health.

Reintroduction and translocation programs were discussed as potential tools for bolstering badger populations, while the benefits of international cooperation in badger conservation were emphasised. The chapter also explored the potential impacts of climate change on badger populations and habitats, as well as key strategies for promoting climate change adaptation in conservation efforts.

Finally, we considered the future challenges and prospects for badger conservation, acknowledging the numerous obstacles that badger populations may face in the coming years. Despite these challenges, the chapter highlights the importance of continued research, community engagement, innovative conservation approaches, strengthened legal protection, and international collaboration in securing a brighter future for badgers and their ecosystems.

In conclusion, badger conservation requires a multifaceted approach that addresses a wide range of interconnected issues. By building on the successes of existing strategies and adapting to emerging challenges, we can work together to ensure the long-term survival and wellbeing of these unique and ecologically important mammals.

Chapter XI: Cultural and Historical Significance of Badger

I. Introduction

Throughout history, the European badger (Meles meles) has held a special place in the symbolism and beliefs of various cultures across Europe. The characteristics attributed to badgers in these cultures often reflect their real-life attributes, such as their resilience, strength, and adaptability.

II. Symbolism and Beliefs

A. Wisdom and Cunning

Badgers have long been symbols of wisdom and cunning in many cultures. Their secretive and nocturnal nature, combined with their elaborate burrow systems, has led to the perception that they possess hidden knowledge and intelligence. This belief is often seen in stories and legends where badgers outsmart larger predators or teach valuable life lessons to humans.

B. Tenacity and Determination

Due to their strong, stocky build and their ability to dig extensive burrow systems, badgers have become symbols of determination and persistence. This symbolism is often reflected in tales of badgers overcoming obstacles or enduring hardships, emphasising their strength of character and unwillingness to give up.

C. Earth and Fertility

As creatures that live close to the earth and have a significant impact on soil aeration and nutrient cycling, badgers have been associated with the earth element and fertility. In some belief systems, badgers are seen as guardians of the earth, helping to maintain balance and ensure the fertility of the land.

D. Protection and Healing

In certain cultures, badgers have been associated with protection and healing. Their natural ability to defend themselves and their underground homes has led to the belief that they possess protective qualities. This symbolism can be seen in charms, amulets, or rituals that incorporate badger imagery to invoke protection or promote healing.

E. Shape-shifting and Transformation

The badger's elusive nature and ability to navigate both above and below the ground has given rise to beliefs in their shape-shifting and transformative powers. In some folklore, badgers are said to possess the ability to change their form, often taking on the guise of humans or other animals.

The rich symbolism and beliefs surrounding the European badger demonstrate the deep cultural connections humans have formed with this remarkable creature. These beliefs and symbols continue to influence modern perceptions of badgers and contribute to the ongoing fascination with these resilient animals.

III. Mythology and Folklore

The European badger (Meles meles) has played a significant role in the mythology and folklore of various European cultures throughout history. These stories and beliefs often portray badgers as symbols of wisdom, resilience, and determination.

A. Celtic Mythology

In Celtic mythology, the badger was considered a brave and tenacious animal, often associated with the warrior class. Some tales depict badgers as guides, leading lost souls through the darkness and into the spirit world.

B. English Folklore

In English folklore, badgers were commonly associated with hard work and industriousness. Tales of badgers digging elaborate underground burrows exemplify their persistence and determination. Badgers also played a role in witchcraft, with some stories describing them as shape-shifting witches or their familiars.

C. Scandinavian Folklore

In Norse mythology, badgers were sometimes linked to the dwarf realm, reflecting their elusive nature and underground habitats. Although badgers are not directly connected to any specific gods in the Norse pantheon, their association with the earth and persistence resonates with the overall themes in Norse mythology.

D. Slavic Folklore

In Slavic mythology, badgers were believed to possess magical powers and were revered for their courage and strength. Some stories even depict badgers as helpers to heroes, aiding them in their quests.

E. Germanic Folklore

In Germanic folklore, badgers were often portrayed as wise and resourceful animals, capable of outwitting larger predators. There are tales of badgers using their cunning to escape danger or teaching important life lessons to humans.

The symbolism and stories surrounding badgers in various European cultures emphasize their resilience, wisdom, and adaptability. These attributes have made badgers an enduring symbol in mythology and folklore across Europe. While attitudes towards badgers have evolved over time, their presence in stories and legends serves as a testament to the deep cultural connections between humans and this fascinating creature.

IV. Folktales and Legends

Badgers have played a significant role in various folktales and legends throughout European history, often reflecting the qualities and attributes that these creatures possess in real life.

A. The Badger and the Fox

In many European folktales, the badger is often portrayed as a wise and cunning character who outsmarts the trickster fox. These stories depict the badger as a clever problem-solver who uses its intelligence to outwit its adversaries and protect its home and family.

B. The Badger and the Moon

In some Slavic legends, badgers are associated with the moon, as their nocturnal lifestyle and underground dwellings are linked with the mysterious and magical aspects of the lunar cycle. These tales often involve the badger helping the moon return to the sky after it has fallen or been stolen.

C. The Badger as a Shapeshifter

In certain Celtic and Nordic tales, badgers are said to possess the ability to transform into other animals or even humans. These stories usually involve a badger that aids a hero in their quest or teaches them valuable life lessons through its transformative powers.

D. The Badger and the Farmer

A common theme in many European folktales involves the badger interacting with human characters, often farmers. In these stories, the badger's wisdom and resilience are used to teach the human characters important lessons about respect for nature, hard work, and the value of persistence.

E. The Badger as a Symbol of Loyalty and Bravery

In some legends, badgers are portrayed as loyal and brave companions to heroes and warriors. Their fierce determination and ability to endure hardships make them valuable allies in battles and adventures.

These folktales and legends showcase the cultural importance and impact of badgers throughout European history. By weaving the badger's natural attributes into the fabric of these stories, the tales serve as a testament to the enduring fascination and respect for these resilient creatures.

V. Badgers in Literature

Throughout the history of literature, badgers have been featured in various works, often as characters that embody their natural traits, such as resilience, intelligence, and resourcefulness. These literary representations have contributed to the broader cultural significance of badgers.

A. Children's Literature

(© Unknown)

Badgers have appeared in numerous children's books, where they often serve as wise, nurturing, or protective figures. Some notable examples include "The Wind in the Willows" by Kenneth Grahame, which features the wise and reclusive Mr. Badger, and "The Tale of Mr. Tod" by Beatrix Potter, in which Tommy Brock, a grumpy badger, plays a central role.

B. Fables and Moral Tales

In Aesop's fables and other moral tales, badgers are often used as symbols to teach valuable lessons. Their resourcefulness and persistence in overcoming obstacles serve as examples for readers to emulate in their own lives.

C. Poetry

Badgers have been featured in various poems that celebrate their unique characteristics and the beauty of the natural world. Poets such as John Clare and Ted Hughes have written verses that capture the essence of badgers and their place in the landscape.

D. Fantasy Literature

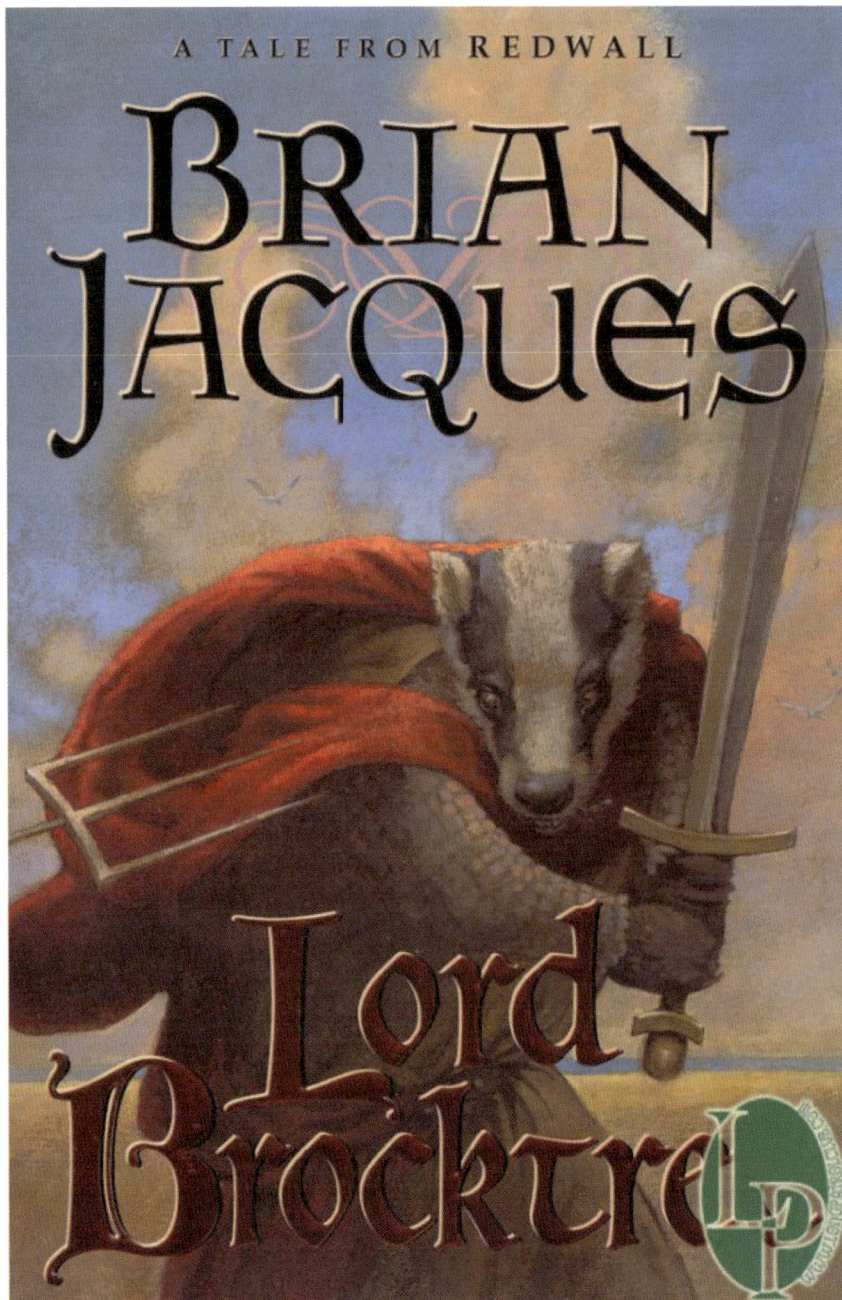

(© Unknown)

In some fantasy novels, badgers are portrayed as magical creatures or as part of mythical worlds. For instance, in Brian Jacques' "Redwall" series, badgers are depicted as fierce warriors and wise leaders.

E. Regional Literature

In literary works that focus on specific regions or cultures, badgers often play a role in reflecting the local folklore and traditions. These stories may highlight the unique relationships between badgers and the people who live alongside them.

The presence of badgers in literature not only showcases their unique qualities but also serves to deepen our understanding of and appreciation for these remarkable creatures. By including badgers in various literary genres, authors have helped to shape the cultural perception of badgers and contribute to their ongoing significance in human culture.

VI. Regional Variations in Folklore

Badgers have held a prominent place in folklore across various regions and cultures, with their roles and symbolic meanings varying from one place to another. These regional variations in folklore demonstrate the cultural adaptability and enduring significance of badgers.

A. British Isles

In Celtic mythology, badgers were considered guardians of the earth and often symbolized strength, perseverance, and determination. In Irish folklore, badgers were sometimes associated with shape-shifting, and certain badger characters could transform into humans. Additionally, in English and Welsh folklore, badgers were seen as wise and resourceful creatures.

B. Scandinavia

In Nordic folklore, badgers were often associated with Thor, the god of thunder, due to their burrowing behaviour and connection to the earth. Badgers were also considered symbols of tenacity, given their reputation for being strong, fierce, and difficult to capture.

C. Eastern Europe

In Slavic folklore, badgers were sometimes considered to be helpful, protective spirits that could ward off evil. They were also believed to possess magical powers, such as the ability to heal illnesses and predict the future.

D. North America

In various Native American cultures, badgers were seen as symbols of courage, persistence, and earth-centred wisdom. Some tribes, such as the Navajo, considered badgers to be protectors and healers, with strong ties to the natural world.

E. Asia

In Japanese folklore, the badger-like creature called "mujina" was believed to possess shape-shifting abilities and was often depicted as a trickster figure. Similarly, in Korean mythology, badgers were considered cunning and resourceful beings with transformative powers.

These regional variations in folklore surrounding badgers reflect the diverse ways in which different cultures have interpreted and related to these fascinating animals. By examining these regional differences, we can gain a better understanding of the cultural and historical significance of badgers and appreciate their enduring impact on human imagination and storytelling.

VII. Ancient Art and Artifacts

The presence of badgers in ancient art and artifacts reveals their significance in various cultures throughout history. These representations provide insight into the roles that badgers played in the lives, beliefs, and stories of people from different times and places.

A. Prehistoric Cave Art

In some prehistoric cave paintings found in Europe, badgers have been depicted alongside other animals, suggesting their importance to early human societies. These images may have been used for storytelling, religious rituals, or as a record of the animals that coexisted with humans during that time.

B. Celtic Art

Badgers have been found in Celtic art, such as on stone carvings and metalwork, often symbolizing strength, perseverance, and connection to the earth. These representations demonstrate the badger's significance in Celtic culture and their reverence for the animal's qualities.

C. Roman Mosaics

In some Roman mosaics, badgers are depicted alongside other animals in scenes depicting hunting or nature. These artistic representations showcase the Romans' appreciation for the natural world and their interest in the various creatures that inhabited it.

D. Medieval Bestiaries

Badgers were often featured in medieval bestiaries, which were illustrated compendiums of animals that combined real observations with symbolic interpretations. The badger's inclusion in these texts highlights its importance in medieval society, where it was believed to possess certain moral and spiritual qualities.

E. Native American Art

Badgers have also been represented in various forms of Native American art, such as pottery, petroglyphs, and totem poles. These artistic depictions demonstrate the important role badgers played in the beliefs and stories of various Native American tribes, often symbolizing courage, persistence, and wisdom.

The study of badgers in ancient art and artifacts allows us to understand their cultural and historical significance across different societies. By examining these artistic representations, we can gain a deeper appreciation for the enduring impact of badgers on human culture and imagination.

VIII. Cultural Evolution of Badger Perceptions

Throughout history, the perception of badgers has evolved in various cultures, shaped by factors such as folklore, mythology, practical uses, and human interaction with the environment. This cultural evolution can be seen in the following stages:

A. Ancient Perceptions

In ancient societies, badgers were often perceived as symbols of strength, persistence, and connection to the earth. Their ability to dig elaborate burrows and adapt to different environments inspired respect and admiration. Badgers were also featured in various myths and legends, reflecting the important role they played in the beliefs and stories of these cultures.

B. Medieval Perceptions

During the medieval period, badgers were depicted in bestiaries and illuminated manuscripts, often imbued with moral and spiritual significance. They were associated with diligence, resourcefulness, and self-reliance, qualities admired by medieval society. However, badgers also began to be seen as pests by farmers due to their burrowing habits, leading to mixed perceptions.

C. Modern Perceptions

As societies progressed and human understanding of nature grew, badgers were increasingly viewed through a scientific lens. People began to appreciate the ecological roles that badgers played in ecosystems, as well as their unique physical and behavioural traits. Simultaneously, badgers continued to appear in literature and art, reflecting their enduring cultural significance.

D. Conservation awareness

With the rise of environmental awareness and conservation movements, badgers have become symbols of the need for human coexistence with wildlife. The challenges faced by badgers, such as habitat loss, persecution, and road casualties, have led to a greater appreciation for their ecological importance and a desire to protect them.

E. Contemporary Perceptions

In today's world, badgers are viewed as complex creatures that embody a range of cultural meanings. They continue to be featured in literature, art, and popular culture, often representing resilience and adaptability. Their role in conservation efforts has also made them a symbol of the importance of protecting biodiversity.

The cultural evolution of badger perceptions demonstrates how our understanding of these creatures has shifted over time, shaped by social, environmental, and historical factors. By examining these changes, we can better appreciate the multifaceted role badgers have played in human culture and the need for continued efforts to protect and coexist with these unique animals.

IX. Badgers as Spiritual Guides

Throughout history, badgers have been regarded as spiritual guides in various cultures and belief systems. These associations can be traced to several key aspects of badger behaviour and symbolism, which have inspired people to view them as possessing wisdom, courage, and grounding energy.

A. Connection to the Earth

As burrowing animals, badgers are intimately connected to the earth. They create extensive underground homes, symbolizing a deep connection to the ground, stability, and the nurturing qualities of Mother Earth. In some indigenous cultures, badgers are seen as guides for connecting to the earth's energy and finding one's roots.

B. Resilience and Persistence

Badgers are known for their determination and tenacity. They are fierce and unrelenting when defending their territory or young, which has led to their association with courage and perseverance. As spiritual guides, badgers can teach people to stand their ground, face challenges with courage, and never give up on their goals.

C. Adaptability

Badgers are highly adaptable creatures that can thrive in various habitats and environments. Their ability to adapt to changing circumstances and find new resources has made them symbols of flexibility and resourcefulness. As spiritual guides, badgers can teach people the importance of adapting to change and embracing new opportunities.

D. Solitude and Self-Reliance

Although badgers are social animals, they also exhibit a degree of independence and self-reliance. They are capable of surviving and thriving on their own, which has led to their association with solitude and introspection. As spiritual guides, badgers can teach people to find strength in solitude, cultivate self-reliance, and reflect on their inner selves.

E. Healing and Transformation

In some cultures, badgers are associated with healing and transformation due to their connection to the earth and their ability to retreat into their burrows for safety and regeneration. As spiritual guides, badgers can help people release negative energies, heal emotional wounds, and transform their lives for the better.

By understanding the symbolism and spiritual significance of badgers, people can draw inspiration and guidance from these resilient creatures. Through their connection to the earth, determination, adaptability, and self-reliance, badgers serve as powerful spiritual guides, offering valuable lessons for personal growth, transformation, and healing.

X. Modern Interpretations

In contemporary society, badgers continue to be featured in various forms of art, media, and popular culture. These modern interpretations not only showcase the enduring appeal of badgers but also reflect changing attitudes and awareness towards wildlife conservation.

A. Art and Design

Badgers have inspired artists and designers who create various forms of artwork, including paintings, sculptures, and illustrations. These artistic depictions often emphasize the beauty and unique characteristics of badgers, highlighting their importance as a part of nature and promoting appreciation for their conservation.

B. Literature and Film

Badgers have been portrayed in numerous books, both for children and adults, as well as in films and television series. These representations often give badgers human-like qualities or use them as allegorical characters to explore themes such as bravery, determination, and the importance of community. Examples include the classic children's book "The Wind in the Willows" by Kenneth Grahame and the popular animated television series "The Animals of Farthing Wood."

C. Mascots and Symbols

Badgers are often used as mascots for sports teams, schools, and organizations, symbolizing strength, tenacity, and resilience. For example, the University of Wisconsin's athletic teams are known as the "Badgers," and the badger is also the state animal of Wisconsin in the United States.

D. Environmental Advocacy

As awareness of conservation issues has grown, badgers have become symbols for broader environmental concerns. Campaigns to protect badgers and their habitats often draw attention to the interconnectedness of ecosystems and the need for a holistic approach to conservation. For example, the Badger Trust, a UK-based organization, actively promotes badger conservation and educates the public about the species' ecological importance.

E. Social Media and Internet Culture

Badgers have also found their way into internet culture, with viral videos and memes featuring badgers garnering widespread attention. These instances not only demonstrate the widespread fascination with badgers but also provide opportunities for raising awareness about their conservation needs.

These modern interpretations of badgers highlight the continued cultural significance of the species and their enduring appeal as symbols of strength, resilience, and connection to nature. Furthermore, they serve as powerful tools for raising awareness about conservation issues and promoting a greater appreciation for the natural world.

XI. Impact on Conservation Attitudes

The cultural and historical significance of badgers can have a substantial impact on conservation attitudes and efforts. By understanding how badgers are perceived in different societies, we can identify key factors that contribute to their protection or endangerment.

A. Public Awareness

The presence of badgers in mythology, folklore, and literature can raise public awareness of the species and its ecological importance. These stories can help foster a connection with the natural world, creating an emotional investment in the protection and preservation of badger habitats.

B. Positive Associations

When badgers are associated with positive qualities such as strength, resilience, and wisdom, they may be more likely to receive public support for conservation efforts. These positive associations can help counteract negative perceptions, such as those stemming from their status as a nuisance species or agricultural pest in certain regions.

C. Cultural Heritage

In some cultures, badgers hold significant historical and cultural value, which can play a crucial role in their conservation. By recognizing the importance of badgers in cultural heritage, communities may be more motivated to protect their habitats and populations, contributing to broader conservation initiatives.

D. Education and Outreach

Cultural and historical associations with badgers can be harnessed to create educational materials and programs that engage the public in conservation efforts. By incorporating stories, art, and mythology, these programs can foster a deeper understanding of badgers and their ecological roles, as well as the challenges they face in the modern world.

E. Advocacy and Policy

The cultural significance of badgers can influence public opinion and policy, leading to more robust conservation measures. For example, societies with strong cultural ties to badgers may be more likely to advocate for legal protection, habitat restoration, and research funding.

F. Community-based Conservation

When local communities value badgers as a part of their cultural heritage, they may be more inclined to participate in community-based conservation initiatives. This involvement can lead to more effective and sustainable conservation efforts, as communities take ownership of the protection and stewardship of badger populations.

XII. Conclusion

The cultural and historical significance of badgers can significantly impact conservation attitudes and actions. By understanding and leveraging these connections, we can foster greater appreciation and support for badger conservation, ensuring the survival and well-being of these unique animals for generations to come.

Chapter XII: European Badger Watching Experiences

(© Alan Woodgate)

I. Introduction

European badger watching offers a unique opportunity for wildlife enthusiasts and nature lovers to observe these fascinating creatures in their natural habitat. Badger watching experiences not only provide a thrilling adventure but also deepen our understanding and appreciation of badgers and their ecological roles. By fostering responsible wildlife observation, we can help protect badgers and their habitats, while simultaneously promoting awareness and engagement in their conservation.

In this chapter, we will explore the process of planning and enjoying a European badger watching trip, providing practical tips and guidelines for maximising the experience. We will delve into the importance of understanding badger behaviour and how it relates to their environment, as well as the safety precautions necessary for both the observers and the badgers. Lastly, we will discuss the significance of sharing these experiences and raising awareness about badgers, ultimately encouraging a deeper connection with nature and fostering an appreciation for these enchanting animals.

II. Planning a European Badger Watching Trip

A successful European badger watching trip requires careful planning and preparation to maximise the chances of spotting these elusive creatures. In this section, we will discuss the various aspects to consider when planning your badger watching adventure.

1. Choose a location: Research the best locations for observing badgers in their natural habitat. National parks, nature reserves, and wildlife sanctuaries with known badger populations are ideal places to start. Additionally, you can consult local wildlife organisations or experienced badger watchers for advice on specific sites.

2. Timing: Badgers are primarily nocturnal, so plan your trip around their active hours, which are typically from dusk until dawn. Keep in mind that badger activity may vary depending on the season, with increased activity during the mating season (February to May) and when raising their young (April to September).

3. Weather conditions: Badgers are more likely to be active during mild, dry weather. Avoid planning your trip during periods of heavy rain or extreme temperatures, as these conditions can discourage badgers from emerging from their setts.

4. Equipment: Bring essential equipment such as a comfortable camping chair or mat, binoculars, a torch with a red filter to minimise disturbances, and suitable clothing for the weather conditions (e.g., waterproofs, warm layers). A camera with a low-light setting can also be useful for capturing the experience without disturbing the badgers.

5. Ethical considerations: Before embarking on your trip, familiarise yourself with the guidelines for responsible badger watching. Avoid causing any disturbance to the animals or their environment, and always respect local wildlife laws and regulations.

6. Learn about badger behaviour: Understanding badger behaviour will greatly enhance your badger watching experience and increase your chances of a successful sighting. Familiarise yourself with badger vocalisations, movement patterns, and signs of sett activity to help you identify potential badger presence.

7. Local knowledge and guided tours: Connecting with local wildlife organisations, badger watching groups, or booking a guided tour can be an excellent way to enhance your experience. Local experts can provide invaluable insights and knowledge to increase your chances of spotting badgers, as well as ensure your trip is conducted responsibly and safely.

III. Maximising the Badger Watching Experience

To make the most of your European badger watching experience, it's essential to follow some guidelines and tips that will increase your chances of success while minimising disturbance to these elusive animals.

1. Arrive early: Reach your chosen location well before dusk to allow enough time for setting up and getting settled. This will also enable you to observe any potential badger activity in the area and make necessary adjustments to your position.

2. Choose a suitable observation spot: Select a vantage point that offers a clear line of sight to the badger sett entrance and foraging areas. Position yourself downwind from the sett to prevent your scent from reaching the badgers, and ensure you have suitable cover to blend into the environment.

3. Remain quiet and still: Badgers have an excellent sense of hearing and can be easily disturbed by sudden movements or loud noises. Keep conversation to a minimum and avoid rustling clothing or equipment.

4. Use appropriate lighting: To minimise disturbance to the badgers, use a torch with a red filter when necessary, as this type of light is less disruptive to their night vision. Avoid shining the light directly at the badgers or the sett entrance.

5. Be patient: Badger watching can require a great deal of patience, as badgers may take time to emerge from their setts or may not appear at all. Stay persistent and enjoy the experience of being immersed in nature.

6. Dress appropriately: Wear comfortable, weather-appropriate clothing in neutral or camouflage colours to blend into the environment. Insect repellent and warm layers are also essential for a comfortable experience.

7. Record your observations: Taking notes or capturing photographs can help you remember your experience and contribute valuable information to local wildlife organisations for monitoring and conservation purposes.

8. Leave no trace: Ensure you take all litter and belongings with you when you leave, and avoid disturbing the badger sett or surrounding environment in any way.

9. Share your experience: Sharing your badger watching experience with others can help raise awareness and appreciation for these fascinating creatures. Connect with other enthusiasts through social media, local wildlife groups, or by participating in citizen science projects.

By following these guidelines and tips, you can maximise your European badger watching experience, fostering a deeper connection with the natural world and contributing to the conservation of these captivating animals.

IV. Safety and Precautions during Badger Watching

To ensure a safe and enjoyable badger watching experience, it is essential to take certain precautions and adhere to guidelines that protect both you and the badgers.

1. Respect wildlife laws and guidelines: Familiarise yourself with local and national wildlife laws to ensure your badger watching activities are legal and in line with best practices. This may include restrictions on visiting certain areas, observing from designated hides, or adhering to specific rules set by landowners.

2. Minimise disturbance: Badgers are sensitive creatures that can be easily disturbed by human presence. Keep a respectful distance from their setts, avoid making loud noises or sudden movements, and use appropriate lighting techniques to minimise your impact on their behaviour and wellbeing.

3. Be aware of your surroundings: When badger watching, it is crucial to remain alert to the environment around you. This includes being conscious of other wildlife, potential hazards (e.g., uneven ground, low branches), and respecting the private property of others.

4. Prepare for the elements: Badger watching often takes place during the evening and night when temperatures can drop significantly. Dress in warm, weather-appropriate clothing, and bring extra layers as needed. Waterproof clothing and sturdy footwear are also recommended.

5. Carry a first aid kit: Accidents can happen, so it's essential to be prepared for emergencies. A basic first aid kit containing items such as plasters, antiseptic wipes, and pain relief medication can prove invaluable in the event of an injury.

6. Inform someone of your plans: Before heading out on a badger watching trip, inform a friend or family member of your intended location and estimated return time. This will ensure someone is aware of your whereabouts in case of an emergency.

7. Be cautious of ticks and insect bites: Ticks can be present in areas where badgers are found, so it is essential to take precautions against bites. Wear long trousers tucked into your socks, use insect repellent, and perform regular tick checks during and after your badger watching experience.

8. Avoid approaching badgers: While badgers are not typically aggressive towards humans, they may defend themselves if they feel threatened. Do not attempt to approach or touch a badger and maintain a safe distance at all times.

By taking these safety precautions and adhering to best practices, you can ensure a secure and enjoyable badger watching experience while minimising any potential risks to both you and the badgers.

VI. Summary and Conclusion

Badger watching can be a truly magical experience, providing an opportunity to observe these elusive and fascinating creatures in their natural habitats across Europe. By following the guidance provided in this chapter, you can plan and execute a memorable European badger watching trip that is both enjoyable and responsible.

Key aspects to consider when planning your badger watching adventure include choosing the right location and time of year, researching local regulations and guidelines, and selecting appropriate equipment to enhance your experience. It is essential to maximise your badger watching experience by understanding badger behaviour, finding suitable vantage points, and practicing patience and perseverance.

Safety precautions and responsible practices are crucial to ensuring that your badger watching activities do not negatively impact badger populations or their habitats. By respecting local laws and guidelines, minimising disturbance to badgers and their environment, and taking appropriate safety measures, you can enjoy an unforgettable experience while contributing to the protection of these captivating animals.

In conclusion, European badger watching offers a unique and immersive wildlife experience that allows you to connect with the natural world and gain a deeper appreciation for the ecology and conservation of badgers. By following the guidance provided in this chapter, you can ensure your badger watching adventure is safe, enjoyable, and leaves a lasting, positive impact on both you and the badgers themselves.

Bibliography

Baines, M. (2017). Badgers: Secrets of the Sett. London: Whittet Books.

Boitani, L., & Powell, R. A. (2012). Carnivore Ecology and Conservation: A Handbook of Techniques. Oxford: Oxford University Press.

Cresswell, P., Harris, S., & Jefferies, D. J. (1990). The History, Distribution, Status and Habitat Requirements of the Badger in Britain. Peterborough: Nature Conservancy Council.

Davison, A., Birks, J., Brookes, R., Braithwaite, T., & Messenger, J. (2002). On the origin of faeces: morphological versus molecular methods for surveying rare carnivores from their scats. Journal of Zoology, 257(2), 141-143.

Delahay, R. J., Smith, G. C., & Hutchings, M. R. (2009). Management of Disease in Wild Mammals. Tokyo: Springer.

Dixon, J. M. (2016). Field Guide to the Badger. London: Whittet Books.

Do Linh San, E., & Crosmary, W. (2016). Badgers (Meles meles). In J. S. Kingdon, D. Happold, T. Butynski, M. Hoffmann, M. Happold, & J. Kalina (Eds.), Mammals of Africa (Vol. 5, pp. 251-258). London: Bloomsbury.

Kruuk, H. (1989). The Social Badger: Ecology and Behaviour of a Group-living Carnivore (Meles meles). Oxford: Oxford University Press.

Larivière, S., & Jennings, A. P. (2009). Family Mustelidae (weasels and relatives). In D. E. Wilson & R. A. Mittermeier (Eds.), Handbook of the Mammals of the World (Vol. 1, pp. 564-656). Barcelona: Lynx Edicions.

Macdonald, D. W., Newman, C., Buesching, C. D., & Johnson, P. J. (2008). Badgers in the rural landscape – conservation paragon or farmland pariah? Lessons from the Wytham Badger Project. British Wildlife, 19(5), 305-312.

Neal, E., & Cheeseman, C. (1996). Badgers. London: T & AD Poyser.

Roper, T. J. (2010). Badger. London: Collins.

Rosell, F., Bozser, O., Collen, P., & Parker, H. (2005). Ecological impact of beavers Castor fiber and Castor canadensis and their ability to modify ecosystems. Mammal Review, 35(3-4), 248-276.

Wilson, D. E., & Mittermeier, R. A. (Eds.). (2009). Handbook of the Mammals of the World: Volume 1: Carnivores. Barcelona: Lynx Edicions.

Woodroffe, R., Macdonald, D. W., & da Silva, J. (1995). Dispersal and philopatry in the European badger, Meles meles. Journal of Zoology, 237(2), 227-239.

Yalden, D. W. (1999). The History of British Mammals. London: T & AD Poyser.

ABOUT THE AUTHOR

Hailing from the enchanting city of Edinburgh, Scotland, I have always been captivated by the diverse and fascinating wildlife that inhabits our beloved homeland. Passionately Scottish and deeply devoted to the study of the natural world, I have focused on researching and understanding the complexities of European badgers, one of Europe's most intriguing creatures.

This passion for wildlife has led to the creation of this comprehensive study, which delves into the lives, habitats, and behaviours of European badgers. As an avid researcher and advocate for wildlife conservation, I have meticulously examined the many aspects of these fascinating animals in order to provide readers with an insightful and authoritative resource.

With this book, I aim to not only inform but also inspire readers to develop a greater appreciation for European badgers and the natural world as a whole. By sharing my knowledge and passion for these captivating animals, I hope to contribute to the ongoing conservation efforts and foster a lifelong love for wildlife in all who read my work.